SOCIAL

JUSTICE

PARENTING

SOCIAL

HOW TO RAISE COMPASSIONATE,

JUSTICE

ANTI-RACIST, JUSTICE-MINDED KIDS

PARENTING

IN AN UNJUST WORLD

Dr. Traci Baxley

HARPER WAVE

An Imprint of HarperCollins*Publishers*

HarperCollins books may be purchased for educational, business, or sales promotional use. For information, please email the Special Markets Department at SPsales@harpercollins.com.

FIRST EDITION

Designed by Nancy Singer

Library of Congress Cataloging-in-Publication Data has been applied for.

ISBN 978-0-06-308236-6

21 22 23 24 25   LSC   10 9 8 7 6 5 4 3 2 1

To my mother, whose love and devotion
both grounded me and allowed me to fly.
To my husband, it is with you that I find belonging.
To my children, my greatest joy.
Always be light and love in the world.

CONTENTS

INTRODUCTION

My husband was driving our three youngest sons—ages six, seven, and nine at the time—to school in his black Toyota Camry when he saw blue lights flash in his rearview mirror. He remained calm and continued talking to the boys while moving from the left-hand lane to the middle lane to allow the police car to pass by. He noticed the cruiser lurch into the right lane—it was now next to him. Glancing over, he was shocked to see the officer shouting at him to pull over. With his eyes on our boys in the back seat, my husband slowly pulled to the side of the road. The police officer got out of his car and approached the passenger side of my husband's car, with his hand over his weapon, screaming, "Roll the goddamn window down."

My husband pushed the control button and as soon as the glass got far enough to show my husband's face, the officer visibly relaxed, moving his hand away from his gun. "Why the hell didn't you pull over when I told you to?" he said. His tone was now one of exasperation, no longer aggressive and threatening. My husband explained he was confused because he wasn't speeding. The police officer then peeked in the back seat at my three brown babies strapped in their seat belts, sitting in wide-eyed silence. The officer looked back at my husband and said, "Do you know what kind of people drive cars like this?"

My husband asked, "Uh, Toyota Camrys?"

The officer snorted and said, "Dark cars with tinted windows."

He looked in the back seat again. "Next time, pull over when you see lights."

That was it. My husband drove off and dropped the boys at school.

My husband is white.

I am a Black mother.

I cried for three days after my husband told me this story. If one of my children encountered the same situation in the future, how would it turn out for them? What would have happened if that officer saw a brown face in the driver's seat instead of a white one?

That incident took place six years ago, and I still feel knots in my stomach every time I think of it. In addition to my constant concern about their safety, I worry about what an experience like this teaches my kids about their place in society. Does it make them feel targeted? Distrustful of others? Like any parent, I want my children to live with more love than fear. I want their childhood to be filled with memories of feeling safe and valued. I want them to know that they belong—freely, unapologetically, and with the power to create change that will make this world better for themselves and others.

How can we do that? How, in this world of injustice, can we give our children this kind of childhood, this sense of their own power?

As any mother can attest, from the moment we learn we're going to have a child, an indescribable feeling of unconditional love takes root. We instantly recognize the potential of this growing human life, and we just as quickly begin to wonder how we can do right by them. How we can teach them to be a good person, to be kind, to do no harm. From the beginning, motherhood is a form of activism.

While this has long been true, the death of George Floyd in May 2020 on the streets of Minneapolis added weight and urgency to our mandate, as we confronted the ugly truths that continue to plague our society. Floyd's last whispering word, "Mama," rang out like a battle cry for mothers everywhere. We could no longer sit in a state of denial, apathy, hyperprotection, or fear. Moms all over the country, the world, became a single, collective maternal force on that brutal day. We knew we could no longer let fear stop us from saving our babies. But what do we do to help our children to feel safe, to prepare them for the sometimes ugly truth?

Many parents are just waking up to the racial, social, and economic inequities of our time, and want to address current events with their young children. More than that, they realize the urgency of the need to be proactive in raising socially conscious children who will be equipped to confront climate change, gun violence, racial injustice, gender discrimination, and economic anxiety. As parents, we are all beginners in some ways. Through trial and error, triumphs and tragedies, we learn to tweak our approach, be more creative, and try new things. This book is intended to serve as another tool in your parenting toolbox. It is not an absolute answer but a road-tested resource.

I am offering my experiences as a mother of five biracial children, educator for three decades, cultural coach for moms and dads, and someone striving to be an openhearted and thoughtful human as I navigate the world in my own skin. In this book, I will have the courage to be vulnerable, open, and honest about my experiences, as a woman and as a mother. These experiences—both the successes and the opportunities to do better next time—have taught me so much and have led me to the work that has culminated in this book. It is based on a parenting philosophy that focuses on creating a space of belonging for yourself and your children, starting in the home and moving outward.

I hope you will explore the pages of this book feeling like we're two friends having a cup of coffee (or, in my case, a cup of green tea), chatting about the world, where our children fit into it, and how we can equip them to leave it better than it was before they arrived. This book is written *with you*, a fellow parent who wants to cultivate more love and a sense of belonging in the world, starting in your own home. This book is an invitation for you to join me in the philosophy and practice of Social Justice Parenting.

I'm excited to begin our parenting journey together.

RADICAL LOVE

I believe in the power of love. *Radical love*. What do I mean by that? I define it as an unconditional love that requires showing up for others, even when it's difficult, and expects nothing in return. It is what drives many of the decisions that I make in my life, particularly how I parent. Radical love focuses on the feelings and perspectives of other people, seeing the humanness inside all of us. It is fueled by compassion and understanding and promotes healing and growth. You can metaphorically hold space for my children, and I can do the same for yours. A mother's radical love is to be willing to struggle with and for others. It challenges us to look at our own biases and expand narrow ways of thinking. It's action-oriented, community-focused, and it creates a space of belonging for everyone. Radical love asks us to lean into our own vulnerabilities, to lead with our hearts, and to be present in our parenting practices.

There is something extraordinary and deeply profound about a mother's laser-focused ability to see a problem, take action, and make change. The word "mom" is a noun, but historically, through cultural and political transformation, its power is manifested as a verb, an action. Moms can be found in the quiet spaces of a child's bedroom teaching self-love and self-agency and on the front lines of a movement advocating for a more peaceful, justice-oriented world.

Of course, there are many dads out there who are actively nurturing and teaching their children to be change agents in the world, and we need you, too. Parenting, in general, includes the purposeful rearing of children to achieve their fullest potential, helping them to find how they will uniquely contribute to the world. Our values and beliefs in our homes are not private; they are the building blocks of everything our children and their generation will spread into the world. Dads play a special role in contributing to their children's growth.

But I believe there is something extraordinary and formidable about a movement of moms. We are cocreating a new cultural paradigm for our children. Moms continue to shift the consciousness of power for impactful change. Moms in action create safe spaces and places of belonging. We build agency and self-advocacy for our children in our homes and our communities. Raising loving, compassionate, conscious children is the ultimate act and reward of activism.

Historically we see the results of moms who moved beyond fear-based parenting and made a lasting impact on society. Mothers Against Drunk Driving (MADD) fights for prevention of and legislation against driving under the influence. Mom Rising mobilizes grassroots action on the most pressing issues facing women, mothers, and families. Moms Demand Action fights for public safety measures to protect people from gun violence. And more recently, the Wall of Moms stood as a human shield between the Black Lives Matter protesters and federal agents around the country during the racial unrest following George Floyd's death.

All of these moms took risks to change the world for their children, for your children, and for my children. Radical love is committed to the struggle of others. It's love magnified. It is love that forgives, accepts, and is always open to hearing and learning and engaging in dialogue.

Radical love is crucial in my interactions with my children, in my commitment to being the best human being I can be, and in how I navigate the world as a woman, as a mother, and as an educator.

This is not to say that I am perfect; I have moments, hours, days that I am not living my truth. But radical love always brings me back in alignment. I regularly ask myself the question: Are you living in, speaking in, reacting in radical love? Are you responding in fear or in courage? Are you choosing silence or action? Are you talking or listening? Radical love is what needs to drive the way we show up for each other right now. Radical love is the foundation on which Social Justice Parenting is built.

This book will support parents who want to live in a world where things are more just, and who want to raise children who will stand up for what is right and fair. The goal of Social Justice Parenting is to raise and nurture a child who can ultimately self-advocate, empathize with others, recognize injustice, *and* become proactive in changing it. As parents, we have no greater responsibility or privilege.

Social Justice Parenting is about showing up for yourself and making sure your children know what it feels like to be loved radically, which allows them to be their authentic, whole selves. It is a movement that requires intentional practices, even when your gut reaction is to shield and overprotect your children. It is a supportive way of raising your children, developing trusting family relationships, and building independence in your children—all while nurturing the humanity of belonging in the world. Ultimately, radical love requires you to think about the impact that your parenting has on my children.

A ROAD MAP

Social Justice Parenting is the road map that I use when I am at a crossroads in my parenting. When I'm lost, I pull out the map. When I'm stuck and confused, I go back to the map. When I'm making hard decisions that have a big impact on my family, I use the map. I developed this program through my work as an educator and my role as a mother, and I continue to turn to it just about every day to guide me through challenging situations.

This book is organized into two sections. Part One outlines what a social justice approach to parenting looks like and what it requires of us. Part Two is where we get into the specific, practical application, giving you concrete parenting tools to put the philosophy into practice. Together, we can raise a better generation.

The building blocks of Social Justice Parenting have gotten me through some tough times and difficult decision making as a mama. I am offering you this road map for when you get lost, or when you are just looking for someone to ride shotgun! I want to share with you how we can do this parenting thing together. It will take all of us, a Village of Moms, a Movement of Moms, who are willing to raise children who care and care deeply. The great news is that we don't have to do it alone. The greater news is that it actually works better when we do it together.

Think of us as a Mosaic of Moms. A mosaic is a clear image created of disparate parts, often mismatched, but that come together to form something beautiful. Like us, each piece is unique, with its own shape and its own history and experiences. Mosaics are often made out of broken glass or shattered pottery . . . and the reality is that sometimes that's what I feel like. When I'm struggling, when I've screwed up and yelled at my kids, or when I just have that feeling of not being enough, it's hard not to feel broken. But the thing is, even in my brokenness, I can come together with all the other women who are just trying to do their best, who also feel broken and frightened, and we can support each other.

We can be fine on our own, but together we are powerful beyond measure. We are stronger than we believe, and each of us has what it takes to raise our children to be compassionate, healthy, confident, and successful. We all have our own way of doing things. But if we bring our individuality together around the common goal of Social Justice Parenting, we're not losing that individuality but *using* it to create something more powerful and inspiring. The brilliance of being surrounded and supported by other moms creates a masterpiece of splendid colors and textures. It can create a better, safer, and more inclusive world for our children.

PART I

CREATING THE BLUEPRINT AND LAYING THE FOUNDATION

CHAPTER 1

WHAT IS SOCIAL JUSTICE PARENTING?

Each time a man stands up for an ideal, or acts to
improve the lot of others, or strikes out against injustice,
he sends forth a tiny ripple of hope, and crossing each
other from a million different centers of energy and
daring those ripples to build a current which can sweep
down the mightiest walls of oppression and resistance.

–Robert F. Kennedy

We are going to have real talks here. I'm not going to present the politically correct or the dressed-up versions of my story. Let's be present, honest, and authentic. I can't ask you to be those things if I'm not doing the same. Showing up this way takes commitment and courage.

Our first courageous act together is committing to doing the work—your reading this book is evidence of that. The second courageous act that I am going to ask of you is to answer an uncomfortable question: Are you parenting from a position of fear and complacency or from courage and radical love? There is no in-between. Either you're stuck in fear or you are evolving to be more present and intentional about how you raise your children and live your life. I usually do not believe in binary thinking, but this is my exception to that rule. So I will ask you again, how are you showing up for your children? Are you an overprotector, or are you a parent who supports problem solving, self-advocacy, and independence?

I've had to ask myself that question more often than I care to tell, but one particular time, it hit me over the head like a sledgehammer.

It was an ordinary Thursday morning. Or at least as ordinary as it got for a family of seven with five school-aged, overscheduled children. I was engaged in my usual morning multitasking: cooking breakfast, giving directives, asking kids to check their morning routine list, and following around my son with ADHD to make sure his teeth and hair got brushed and that his backpack was actually going to make it in the car that morning—organized chaos at its finest! What I didn't notice at the time was that my oldest son was not in the kitchen. This may not seem like a reason to panic; it had only been a few minutes since I last saw him. But our family had just entered a new journey, one that we were still figuring out how to navigate.

My oldest son, then thirteen, had recently been diagnosed with anxiety, and what might otherwise seem like "normal" situations and surmountable obstacles had become grounds for concern and sometimes outright panic. I was used to his need to immediately master any skill as a small child or his insistence that a grade of 95 percent on his assignments in middle school wasn't good enough to get him into Ivy League schools. I had learned to parent him when he came to me distressed because he forgot to do a problem on his homework or missed a basket during his basketball game. I had always been his champion, his go-to person, his rock. I understood him (honestly, there's a little of me in him). He knew I was his wind, his calm, his safe place. Although challenging at times, supporting him was one of my greatest joys. But as his anxiety began to increase, his reactions became more and more intense and irrational. As his Black male body got taller and took up more space, and as I watched so many moms lose their Black boys at the hands of others, my small concerns slowly turned into paralyzing fear.

On this ordinary Thursday morning, while I was completing my usual "getting it all done morning routine," my son realized that he had forgotten to do one of his homework assignments. I said, "It's not that big of a deal, do what you can on the way to school and turn in what you've completed. Next time you'll know to be more organized with your planner." I'm normally a big proponent of natural consequences, but he's a straight-A student whose grades wouldn't suffer too much for one partially incomplete worksheet. Unfortunately, however, my son was veering into full panic mode. I knew he was upset, but I wanted him to deal with the situation on his own, using some of the coping strategies we'd worked on together, and come up with a reasonable solution. At that point, I walked away to finish the morning routine.

And here is where the ordinary Thursday morning became extraordinary. As we were piling into the car heading for school drop-offs, I asked my three youngest boys, "Where is your brother?" I heard a resounding chorus of "I don't know." So I politely blew the horn and waited. Nothing. I waited another minute; this time, I felt my blood beginning to boil as I looked at the clock in the car. I honked again, this time a little longer, a little louder, not as polite—still nothing. So I got out of the car and headed back into the house.

I was beginning to lose control. As I opened the door, I screamed my son's name (not my best mommy moment) and told him to get in the car. Sending my children out into the world with me screaming at them is usually a deal breaker for me—it's simply not done. But there I was, screaming! "Get over this homework nonsense and get out here; you are going to make everyone late." I went to his room, opened the door, and screamed, "Let's go!" No one was there.

At that moment, my anger started to dissipate, and my own panic was kicking into high gear. I was running throughout the house, screaming his name, and all I could hear was dead silence. My anxiety had now escalated into complete fear. I knew he was upset. I knew he was struggling. I knew my kid better than anyone, better than he knew himself. Why didn't I actively listen this morning? So many questions were going through my mind as I ran from room to room, kicking doors open, violently turning on lights.

My inner mean girl was rearing her ugly head. "Why didn't you show more compassion and kindness? Why didn't you practice a little more radical love this morning? You are a terrible mom!" she said to me. I got to my bedroom, the only room left in the house to check and he wasn't there. I swung open the door of the small, dark, walk-in closet, and my body just gave in. My son, my Black teen son, in a state of anxiety and possibly irrational thinking (and wearing his school hoodie), was now walking or running somewhere in my predominantly white neighborhood. I fell onto my knees in fetal position and just screamed, *"Why wasn't I more kind? Where was my radical love? Did I do enough?"*

I know some of you are still asking why this was such a big deal. "What is she talking about? Is what enough?" And then there are some of you reading these words and experiencing a tightening in your chest or a sting in your eyes . . . you know exactly what I am talking about. Any parent who has a child who has been marginalized due to race, ethnicity, ability, mental illness, sexual orientation, religion, gender, or language recognizes the total sense of overwhelm that I felt that ordinary Thursday on the floor of my closet.

Home should be a safe place. A place where you are heard and valued and unconditionally loved. I know the world isn't always kind to kids who look like my son. That moment of fear, as the mother of my Black son, was paralyzing. Did I teach him enough to stay safe in the world? Why isn't the world a safe place for him?

Did he know his worth in the midst of all the fears in our country surrounding his Black boy body . . . and at that moment of my fear, was one of my white neighbors having *their* fears when he walked past their house? Did he listen to me all those times we had "the talk" about how to respond to law enforcement, how to look less intimidating in his six-foot Black male frame? Did he remember what we discussed about the "stand your ground" law here in Florida? Why wasn't I more kind? Why didn't I do more?

As parents, many of us have times when we feel like we've failed. That Thursday morning, I felt like a failure. In that moment on my closet floor, I was parenting from a place of fear. I needed to find a way to transform that negative space into more positive energy, energy that could have a rippling effect or impact beyond my family and into the world. I needed something to help me move through the debilitating fear.

That morning was a defining moment. Right then, I was clear on the mission, though I was fuzzy regarding the plan. I knew I had to do more than have conversations with my children about staying safe. That wasn't enough. I needed to know that other mothers were having these conversations with their children, too. I needed to know that other mothers were teaching their children about the injustices that my children will face because of the color of their skin. I needed to know that mothers who didn't look like me would still see my children as part of a global village and would take care of them as their own. That moment, on my closet floor, I was thinking of you, dear reader. I was thinking about how complicated it feels to try to raise our children to be open-minded, compassionate, knowledgeable about the world, and positioned to make a difference. It sounds simple enough, right? But those daily decisions can be scary and overwhelming. On that ordinary Thursday, Social Justice Parenting was created.

WHAT IS SOCIAL JUSTICE PARENTING?

I think one thing that we can all agree on is that we want to leave this world in better shape than when we got here. Social Justice Parenting is my way of contributing to that cause. And yet, as much as I want to support other families, this book is also a selfish endeavor. It's as much about keeping my children safe as it is about giving you the tools you need to empower your children to be more socially conscious. As a mom of color, I know I can't do that alone. I need moms (and dads) who don't look like me to incorporate Social Justice Parenting in their homes for my children—my daughter but particularly my four Black sons—to feel safe, to feel valued, and to have a sense of belonging in the world.

One value that my husband and I have always agreed on, as we grew our family, is being open and honest with our children when it comes to the realities of the world around them. (I plead the Fifth on Santa Claus and the tooth fairy.) When it comes to significant issues and hard questions, we generally don't shy away from them; we take this responsibility of parenting very seriously.

I often hear from parents that they want to keep their children in a bubble, protecting their innocence as long as possible. One mom, with tears in her eyes, told me she didn't want to discuss the social issues that exist "out there" in her home. When many of my affluent white mom coaching clients begin working with me, they say they are going to wait as long as possible (or until their child asks) to talk about "those" topics. My typical response is, "Aren't you lucky you get to choose?"

Many children don't have the choice of living in that bubble, not even for a minute. My kids certainly don't. The good news is that in the wake of nationwide calls for social justice, many moms have begun to realize that this idea of a bubble of innocence isn't extended to every child and is a function of privilege. More and more, I'm receiving proactive inquiries from these moms: "Tell me what to do." "Show me how to engage in this dialogue." "Help me teach my children to know more and do better." They've realized that their bubble keeps children from the truth. You can't practice anti-racism in a bubble.

So I'll ask again, are you parenting from a place of fear or radical love? When you say you are an ally or an activist, but you still want to keep your children in the protected, fear-based bubble, then you need to question what that means for you and your family. You cannot be an ally and parent from fear.

As a mama engaged in Social Justice Parenting, it is my responsibility to make sure my children are aware of what's going on in the world and that it's our responsibility as a family, as human beings, to educate ourselves on how issues "out there" impact others. The only way that we can contribute to a world that's more peaceful, loving, and inclusive is to do work that highlights and exposes where we fit into it (our privileges and pain points) and consider how we can be of service to others. If we only discuss events and topics from our privileged existence, we are not allowing our children to grow in ways that embrace other perspectives and seek to solve problems. For society's awareness/consciousness to transform, we need everyone— parents of color, white parents, wealthy parents, those living in economic poverty, ethnically diverse parents, parents of children with disabilities—to be willing to raise our little ones to see the value and humanity in us all.

I totally understand that each of you wants what's best for your children. So you should! But Social Justice Parenting means you also want (and take actions toward) what's best for *all* children. Social Justice Parenting requires you to engage in dialogue with your children about what's going on in the world beyond your front door or gated community. It involves modeling and taking action to change the things that marginalize, hurt, or stereotype others. This is our job as parents. I believe in the power of radical love, and I remain hopeful that we will raise a generation of children who are more socially conscious and compassionate than ever. So let's push past the fear and dive in.

FROM FEAR TO RADICAL LOVE

As parents, many of us worry about how we can most effectively influence the well-being of our children. Add to those fears our concerns about the environment in which they're growing up—including the divisions in our country and the social issues that keep us awake at night—and it's hard not to be anxious about our children's futures. At the time I'm writing this, my family is quarantining in the midst of a global pandemic. Our country is at a political and social crossroads.

Current social issues rooted in racism, sexism, and the denial of basic human dignity are causing many parents to feel hopeless and fearful. Politicians, the media, and ordinary citizens are hurling heated rhetoric across the aisle, all of which is fueling fear. The intolerance of differences continues to cause communities to mistrust and isolate themselves from one another. In an overwhelming and primal effort to shield and protect our children, many parents have become hypervigilant and overprotective.

No one *wants* to be a helicopter parent. None of us consciously realizes when we're smothering our children in bubble wrap. But our anxieties for our children—that they aren't hurt physically or emotionally, that they become successful, that they do as well as other children—can cause us to parent out of fear. We make ourselves believe that if they get one bad grade, then they won't get into a good college . . . and then they won't be able to get a good job or have a successful career or live a good life. We spiral into assigning terrifying consequences for every tiny misstep. And we begin to doubt our own abilities as parents.

The problem is that these fears get passed on to our children. Our fears of not being enough get translated through our parenting, and our children take them on. Anxiety runs in families, with 80 percent of children of anxious parents reporting anxiety themselves.[*] Some of that may be genetic, but consider this: If you transmit to your children that the world is not a safe place, and that they are not able to handle it on their own, is it any surprise that they would feel anxious? How does it support them in becoming capable adults if we teach them that they are *not* capable?

In the current political climate, more and more parents are feeling a sense of paralyzing fear. Recent surveys have found that parents' top fears for their children consistently include:

The fear that their child will be hurt or attacked

The fear that their child won't feel safe in the world

The fear that their child will be bullied

The fear that their child will grow up with a sense of entitlement

---

[*] G. S. Ginsburg and M. C. Schlossberg, "Family-Based Treatment of Childhood Anxiety Disorders," *International Review of Psychiatry* 14, no. 2 (2002): 143–54.

This feeling of not being safe often causes parents to micro-manage their child's every move and every decision. Listen, I get it. I find myself micromanaging my kids in certain situations, en-suring they are successful and safe and that the world is kind to them. I call it the "mama-bear syndrome." (That sounds much better than micromanaging, don't you think?) But what if we harness that fear into action, so *all* of our children have the opportunity to feel safe and secure? What if, as former president Barack Obama said, we are the ones that we are waiting for? We are the change that we seek?

When we are afraid, we are less rational, which complicates the already overwhelming task of raising children. This is why we have to make conscious choices about where we want to stand at the end of the day. We have to put our core values first. Our hearts may feel fear in walking down this road. Our hearts may tell us to protect our babies, to keep them safe, to shelter and shield them from the ugly truths in the world. Our hearts may feel the burden of choosing what we believe is right. When we attempt to move beyond fear, we step into what feels like quicksand. We feel it and our children feel it, too.

Emotions are infectious—particularly fear and anxiety. And while these emotions intensify among us all, children are the most vulner-able. Children sometimes find it difficult to detach their angst from their parents' stress, and parents have a difficult time controlling their stress in the presence of their children, especially during crises. Ac-cording to UNICEF, American children rank in the bottom quarter among developed nations in well-being and satisfaction with their lives. We parents are partly to blame, raising children in a protective bubble to shelter them from disappointment and harm. But in our primal effort to shield our offspring from the ugliness of the world, we may inadvertently imprint on them, infecting them with our own anxieties. Our intention is to protect them, but what we often end up doing is adding to their feelings of hopelessness by not giving them tools to deal with the things that they see as unfair. We may also make it more difficult for them to empathize with the struggles of people who are different from them.

I want to raise children who are safe, well adjusted, independent, kindhearted, and joyful. I want to live in a world where things are more just and fair for everyone, raising children who will stand up when injustice is present for anyone. If these sound like parent goals, please raise your hand (both of my hands are in the air). I want to live in and create a world in which my children can be their true, authentic selves. I want to model for my children the best of humanity and lean into those parts of myself that need more work, and, in the famous words of Maya Angelou, to do the best that I can until I know better, and when I know better, to do better.

If you have chosen to read this book (and I am grateful you did), these statements must ring true for you. We are at a crossroads, family. We know we can do better. It's time. Our children are depending on us to move beyond the fear.

THE FOUNDATION OF A SOCIAL JUSTICE HOME

A Social Justice Home is made up of commitments that you make to yourself and to your children about the way you want to show up as a team. It holds great promise within its walls, a promise that speaks to the things that are important and the ways in which your family can make a difference in the world. It speaks to the way you value your children and how they value themselves and others. There's a saying in sports, "you play the way you practice," which can also be applied to parenting. The values and actions we practice at home will be reflected in the way our children move through the world. Social

Justice Homes are built on a strong foundation of qualities that tran-
scend four walls.

A Social Justice Home is . . .

**Grounded in the lives, interests, and experiences of each family
member.** We must provide space in the home for the lives and experiences of each of our children—which requires getting to know them
and taking an interest in what engages them. It can be easy to fall
into prioritizing one family member over another; I know that when
my son with ADHD was struggling in school and we were working
on getting a diagnosis, a great deal of my attention was wrapped up
in him. At times this can't be avoided, and it is in fact appropriate—if
one member of the family is in crisis or simply in need of a little extra
attention, then we should absolutely give them what they need. But
in general, we need to make sure that each and every member of the
family feels like they belong and that they are appreciated and valued
and a part of the greater whole.

That extends to the adults in the family, as well. It can be so easy
for parents to become wrapped up in our children's lives, often to the
detriment of our partnerships (again both hands raised here). I am
totally guilty of this. Some days I treat my husband like my business
partner or my assistant. My infamous texts: "I need you to pick up
at 6:00 from basketball. We need more eggs and toilet paper. Did
you bring the garbage can to the curb before you left for work?" All
followed by a kissing emoji face, as if that makes it all better! The fact
is that it is so important to give space to adult needs and interests,
too, and not just for the health of the relationship but also to help our
children understand that parents are people, too.

Pro-justice and empathetic. It may seem a little obvious to say that
a Social Justice Home is pro-justice . . . but the fact is that it can be

easy to lose sight of what that means. When I say pro-justice, I don't just mean giving each person what they need to be successful in the home, although that is certainly part of it. The intention is to call out the need to be proactive about justice, both inside and outside the home.

Justice, in this context, means choosing to do the right thing, even when it's difficult. There's a difference between being a "good person" and being pro-justice. One of my clients struggled with this concept with her partner. She wanted to raise anti-racist children and her husband thought raising "good people" was enough. Raising good people may, for example, include teaching your children that bullying someone is wrong. They know not to pick on the kid who is different. But do they stand up for that kid when other children are abusive? This isn't easy, particularly not in the complex and cliquey worlds of middle and high school. It requires a strong moral center and the courage to do what is right.

The difference between being a "good person" and being "pro-justice" is action. Being a good person is passive, but being pro-justice requires being empathetic and courageous, both of which can be taught and modeled in your home. When I talk with my children about being pro-justice, we unpack what that means and what it looks like. Pro-justice for whom? The answer, always, is *everyone*. Our children have to be able to empathize with and work against all forms of discrimination—whether it's based on race, gender, weight, sexual orientation, or any other of the numerous ways we humans separate ourselves from one another. We have to give them the tools to recognize and dismantle injustices.

Reflective and dialogic. Conversation, collaboration, and communication are how we stay plugged in to each other and the world around us. This isn't easy; it takes work and effort, and it's something we as parents struggle with in our daily lives, too. It's a constant process, but the way we get better at it is by thinking about it and talking about it. And acting on it.

Sometimes one of my kids will come home with a story about something that happened at school. They'll tell me that a classmate was treated poorly and share how that made them feel, especially when they may have been afraid or made the decision not to say anything. Because I believe in the power of having dialogue and teachable moments, I try to create space to talk about it. I also love those moments when I walk into one of the kids' bedrooms and I see that they're lying on the bed with one of their siblings already talking it out with each other. I quietly close the door and walk away, smiling and basking in their ability to show empathy and kindness while guiding their brother or sister back to our core values with radical love. This is when I am most proud. This is when I know that I have truly created a Social Justice Home.

Accountable. Conversation and collaboration naturally lead to accountability. Every member of a Social Justice Home supports the others in their efforts to be pro-justice. We are encouraging and positive . . . but we also hold each other's feet to the fire. In my famous line around the house, "you need to own your own junk first," my kids know they have to take responsibility for their own actions or the part that they played in a situation—and so do their dad and I! When you know you have eyes on you—loving, supportive eyes, but eyes nonetheless—you tend to pay more attention to what you do. You put more thought into your actions each day, and over time you begin to develop positive habits.

One that acknowledges we are all in process. Social justice is not something that will be achieved overnight. Just as our society is in process, so are we. The work of creating belonging is always changing because the people you are creating belonging for are forever evolving—at least that's the goal, right? There will be ups and downs. Don't be afraid of getting it wrong because that puts us right back in the paralyzing state of fear. We aren't going back there. A Social Justice Home is a safe place where each of us acknowledges that mistakes happen. We pick each other up when we fall and help make a plan to do better next time. Creating a Social Justice Home starts with *you*. You are its foundation, as you set the example for what this looks like. But remember, this doesn't mean you have to be perfect! It means that you continue to live in radical love, for yourself as much as you do for your children, learning and growing along the way.

THE ROCKS OF SOCIAL JUSTICE PARENTING

That moment on my closet floor was when I began to transform fear into decisive action. You can begin the transformation too and it starts with you remembering one word: ROCKS.

Some of you may be familiar with crystal therapy . . . there is a belief that specific stones contain different energy vibrations. There is a group of rocks that have grounding, protective energy. These rocks, like hematite, smoky quartz, and jasper, absorb negative energy from your body; they bring you calm in moments of stress or worry. From the lens of Social Justice Parenting, I want you to see yourself as one of these grounding rocks for your children, able to absorb their negative energy.

Here's another visual. Picture water flowing down a shallow stream . . . let's say that flow of water represents fears, yours and those of your children. If you put a few rocks in the stream, let's call them rocks of radical love, the rocks will displace the water—displace the fear. What if we put those rocks of radical love right in the middle of that flow of fear? They will change the direction of the water's flow, causing rippling and expansive changes in the energy of the river.

Why am I using rock metaphors? Because at the heart of Social Justice Parenting is the acronym ROCKS. Our ROCKS are the building blocks we place on the foundation. They make up the essential qualities of a pro-justice home.

Reflection. You must be able to reflect on your prior experiences, values, and childhood memories to uncover how they shaped the way you see the world and their impact on the way you approach parenting.

Open Dialogue. Nothing is off-limits. It's essential to engage in hard conversations with your children about issues that impact your family and your community.

Compassion. Regarding others—and ourselves—with compassion is critical to being pro-justice.

Kindness. I often say kindness is compassion in action. We need to model what kindness looks like for our children and the joy that the receiver and the giver both experience with positive acts.

Social Justice Engagement. This represents the forms of activism in which your family participates to make changes in your community and the world.

We have to make ripples where we can and impact the places and spaces we occupy. If we all did this, perhaps the ripples of radical love would be felt in the massive river of social injustice. The rest of the book will show you how to actively create opportunities to connect your family's life with broader and deeper issues in the world. Social Justice Parenting can help you lean into your children's natural curiosities and desire to connect. Together, we can create a generation that puts humanity first and individual power and privilege last.

The story that left off on my closet floor has a happy ending, by the way. Thirty minutes later, as I drove around looking for him, I found my son. He was calm and walking just outside our community. As I pulled up next to him in my car, he said, "Hey, Mom. I was really scared about the impact on my grade. I just needed some space and fresh air to work through it. I had my phone on the entire time, and I'm sorry if I scared you. I'm okay." All I could do was smile and breathe. I was so happy and grateful to see him.

JOURNAL WRITING

Consider your fears as a parent. Write them down, and then reflect on each fear. Where did it come from? Is it a rational fear? Remember, you have to name your fears before you can overcome them. Now is your chance.

_____

_____

_____

_____

_____

_____

CHAPTER 2

THE NEED TO BELONG

A deep sense of love and belonging is an irreducible need
of all people. We are biologically, cognitively, physically, and
spiritually wired to love, to be loved, and to belong. When
those needs are not met, we don't function as we were
meant to. We break. We fall apart. We numb. We ache. We
hurt others. We get sick.

—Brené Brown

Some of my first memories of belonging began in my childhood.
I lived in a very tight village of Black families, friends, and community love. Every family on the three streets that made up our
neighborhood knew one another and looked out for each other's
children. The streets were filled with sweaty children playing tag
and hide-and-seek, having sleepovers, hanging out at Tuck's Community Center, and visiting the "lilly-dillie" lady's house, where we
could buy frozen fruit juice treats—a dime for a small Dixie cup, or
a quarter for a large refuge from the summer heat. We would sit outside, licking our icy lilly-dillie delights, sticky syrup dripping down
our arms. Life was as sweet as the lilly-dillies we crunched on the
doorsteps of our friends' houses. We were loved and scolded by every
mother in the neighborhood; it was indeed a village of aunties and

othermothers making sure we were all safe, happy, and fed. I have lovely childhood memories of the lifetime friendships that I made (and still have) with many of the children and families in Carver Park.

When I was in third grade, my mom married my stepdad. I thought it was great that my mom and stepdad were getting married until I found out that we would be moving into his house, which was in the city north of my neighborhood cocoon. I was leaving my all-Black community, where I felt true radical love—safe, accepted, valued. In her book *Braving the Wilderness*, Brené Brown tells us that "true belonging doesn't require you to change who you are; it requires you to be who you are." In that community, in that neighborhood, I could be me. I knew who I was, and I knew I belonged there.

Leaving the place where I was so sure I belonged was devastating in many ways. Not because I had to leave the only friends that I've ever known, but mostly because I moved to a neighborhood where we were the single Black family. No more running from house to house with my friends, no more walking to the community center, and no more lilly-dillies!

This, I believe, began my life's passion of finding radical love and belonging for everyone.

As a relatively outgoing child, and active in sports, it didn't take me long to make friends at my new school. Don't get me wrong; it wasn't always easy. The children in the neighborhood constantly reminded me that I was "different" from everyone else. I was often othered. I didn't have the vocabulary to name it at that time, but I certainly knew I felt it. I've held on to some unkind memories, like when a group of boys in my new neighborhood said, "You're burnt! God left you in the oven too long." Or when I was hanging out with friends at a high school party who were openly making racist comments about Black people. When I turned to them with a look of disbelief, they quickly said, "Oh no, not you . . . you're different!" This explanation was meant to somehow excuse their behavior, as if I should appreciate their backhanded "compliment."

Another time, a group of Black students who were bused into my high school from the neighboring city (the one my family sadly left) asked me why I talked "white," and if I thought I was better than them because I lived in Boca. They told me I was an Oreo (black on the outside, white in the middle). I wanted to say, "I'm still me . . . still one of you, aren't I?" but I wasn't brave enough to speak out, to tell my truth, and honestly, I didn't think they would have really cared to hear it.

It wasn't just those mixed messages from the outside; I also received similar contradictions in my home. My dad's experiences of the civil rights movement and Jim Crow laws informed the way he saw the world and, consequently, how he raised us. Although we lived in an all-white neighborhood, my dad, because of his experiences, had a hard time completely trusting white people in general. He continuously hammered into our heads, "Be careful; you can't trust the White Man." "No, you can't have sleepovers at her house." "Don't get too close to her." My nine-year-old brain could not understand this concept at all. You took me out of my safe Black village, and you put me in a place where I'm surrounded by a sea of white people, and you don't want me to trust them? Huh? How does that work?

My parents preached that being equal to my white peers was not enough. I had to be better, faster, stronger than them just to be seen as good enough. I think this mindset has led to success in my life, but I also believe my battle with imposter syndrome as an adult in higher education and as an entrepreneur is a direct reflection of these constant struggles between the two worlds. It's similar to the debate that historians have regarding the impact of desegregation. It was great in many ways, affording more equitable resources in schools. But it also damaged the Black community and culture in irreparable, unforeseeable ways.

Looking back, I understand why my parents decided to move our family. My sisters and I had a wonderful childhood and we were afforded many opportunities. My mom was, and remains, literally the wind beneath my wings. Her love, compassion, and dedication to my sisters and me continue to sustain me every day. She is the most amazing woman, my role model in all that I do. Moving us to the new neighborhood was like "moving up" in many ways—bigger house, expansive yard, schools with more resources, among other benefits. My parents wanted more for us than they had, and this new neighborhood was part of that. It opened up possibilities we wouldn't have had otherwise.

I learned to speak the language and discover the behaviors of those in power. I learned to code-switch and live, as Black feminist Patricia Hill Collins says, as the outsider-within. I was very successful in school. I had good grades, played several sports, and was the captain of the cheerleading squad and soccer team. I was on the student council, the leadership team, and I was homecoming queen. I prided myself on not attaching to one particular group. I had friends who were athletes, in theater, the academically successful kids, and the popular kids (both Black and white). Again, looking back, I see my passion for belonging. It was always there; it drove me then and continues to drive me as a mother, as an educator, as an equity and inclusion consultant and parenting coach. I know these and other experiences were instrumental in what drives me in the work that I do and the impact that I want to have in the world.

BELONGING IS A BASIC HUMAN NEED

There's a theory of psychology known as Maslow's hierarchy of needs, which includes what humans require to live their lives fully. Each lower need must be met before successfully moving to the next level. In this hierarchy, belonging ranks third, just after physical needs like food, shelter, water, and safety. The need to belong is primitive and is a vital component of our well-being throughout our lives. When this need is not met, we experience emotional and physical distress. Though we aren't often taught the importance of belonging, we are born hardwired with the need to be cared for, valued, and supported. As parents, we do everything in our power to make sure our children find friends, teams, schools, and other groups where they feel good about themselves and they feel a sense of belonging and acceptance. It's heartbreaking when your child tells you they were left out, or feel alone, or that they don't fit in. I cried for ten days straight the day one of my sons, who was then in seventh grade, told me he ate lunch by himself at school most days. I know you felt the sting in your belly as you read that. That was six years ago and it still makes my eyes tear up.

I can recall my daughter's first experience with the confusion and hurt of not belonging. Our town has a large Jewish community. When my daughter was in kindergarten, many of her classmates, including her closest friend, were Jewish. After school one day, Alexandra got into the car and began sobbing as I tried to quickly, but safely, get out of the car pickup lane. "Do I need to pull over to go back into the school to confront somebody about something?" I asked. "What's wrong, Alexandra? What happened?" Finally, through her sobs, she said, "I'm not Jewish. Why can't I just be Jewish?"

With some relief, I decided I didn't have to go swarm the principal's office on this one. I could handle it on my own. I pulled the car over and let her get all the hurt out. Apparently earlier that day at recess, one of the girls in her class told Alexandra and another classmate that they couldn't play with them today because they were Christians. We talked about what it meant to be Jewish, religiously and culturally. We talked about how wonderfully made she was and all the attributes that made her unique, including all the cultural groups that run through her own veins. We also talked about loving yourself, speaking up for yourself, and finding friends that love you for who you are. Then we called her best friend, who happened to also be Jewish, and made a playdate.

I recently asked Alexandra if she recalled this kindergarten incident and she replied, "I don't, but I do remember the same girl was always touching my hair, calling it marshmallow in sixth grade until I screamed at her to stop and I got in trouble with the teacher." I remember that incident as well. It was the second week of middle school and she got off the bus, came in the house, and leaned her back against the inside of the front door and cried. That incident solidified my daughter's hate affair with her curly hair for the next several years. She just wanted to belong. To be and look like everyone else. I couldn't change or protect her from every situation in the world, but I did have more control over what happened inside my home. I did my best to make her feel safe, loved, and accepted at home. I didn't always get it right, but I am hopeful that I was more often right than wrong.

When children grow up with a sense of belonging, they have an easier time creating and maintaining relationships, managing stress, and functioning in the world as adults. Sometimes when people lack feelings of being grounded, being centered and connected, they can self-sabotage and make harmful choices. These choices then lead to aggressive behaviors and bullying, as hurt people hurt people. And, conversely, the children they tend to bully also suffer from poor self-esteem. One out of every five students in the United States reports being bullied,* but here's the thing: Both the bullies and the children being bullied suffer from the same lack. They both feel like they don't belong and are disconnected from their peers and sometimes from their families as well.

As I write this, we are all collectively separated from one another, socially distancing to preserve our health and safety. This pandemic has taken its toll in so many ways, not least of which is the way it has eroded our sense of belonging. I have watched as my children have struggled to maintain their sense of belonging with their peers, trying to learn and socialize through videoconferencing and texting (okay, they always texted, but still). It's hard not to worry about what this enforced isolation is doing to our kids, but my hope is that, somehow, this shared experience will actually help create a collective sense of belonging—we may be alone, but at least we're all going through it together. There's something comforting in sharing difficult experiences together. This pandemic has brought heartbreak, but it has also shown us the healing power of love.

BELONGING THROUGH LOVE

I recall my first teaching job, fresh out of my master's program. There was a hiring freeze in the middle of the school year, but one teacher decided she wasn't coming back after the holiday break, leaving her class without a teacher in January. Guess who got hired for that class? As I met other members of the faculty on the preplanning day, before the students arrived, they shook their heads, touched my shoulder, or said "Good luck." Once the children arrived back to school, I

---

* PACER's National Bullying Prevention Center, "Bullying Statistics," https://www.pacer.org/bullying/resources/stats.asp.

understood why they had such empathy for me and why I was the
only teacher offered a job during the hiring freeze.

His name was Rubin.

Rubin was a small, thin African American child, born from a
mom who was addicted to crack and alcohol. He would often scream
and kick during the school day, I believe due to both physical and
emotional pain. He was what we in education call a "runner," which
basically meant that at any time he might bolt to the door and run out
the door into the parking lot, out into the street, wherever. I would
have to push the intercom button to the front office and get someone
on the leadership team to come find him or catch him before he left.

Rubin was surprisingly strong. Some days it would take the principal, the guidance counselor, and me to hold him down. I would go
home at night sobbing. My heart was so heavy for him, for the rest
of the class, and, honestly, for myself. I wanted to be an effective
teacher. I wanted to create a community of little ones who loved each
other and felt safe together. I was struggling with that. I was struggling with Rubin. His mom was struggling with her addictions. And
most painful of all, Rubin was struggling with just surviving in his
own skin.

I decided that I was no longer going to buzz the office for help. I
had to figure it out on my own, because the more I asked for support,
the more often Rubin, who was already academically behind (didn't
know any letters or numbers and couldn't recognize his own name),
would be pulled out of the class and miss more lessons with me. So
one morning, I pulled Rubin aside and said, "Listen, we are going to
do this differently. I don't want to call the office anymore. I am going
to support you and we are going to get through all of this together. Is
that okay with you?" Rubin, not completely sure what I was talking
about, reluctantly nodded his head and slowly went to hang his backpack on the hook.

During story time later that morning, Rubin started his shaking and I knew the screams were next, which could ultimately lead to him bolting out of the door. I asked one of my students to please lock the door. I kept reading aloud to my class. I sat next to Rubin, still reading my story. I gave the book to my assistant who was visually getting nervous and moving toward the intercom buzzer on the wall. I slowly but very deliberately shook my head and asked her to keep reading to the children. I put Rubin on my lap, wrapped my legs around his, and gave him a tight bear hug and he screamed and kicked and his body stiffened up. We did this every day for two and a half weeks. Some days my assistant would take over reading or explaining a lesson; some days I taught while holding Rubin. During the mid-nineties, there was no special training for teachers to support a child like Rubin. All I could think to do was love, so I just loved up on him.

It was on the seventeenth day of not calling the administration, of temporarily locking the door, of teaching lessons while loving on Rubin, that he said to me, "I feel it when it's coming on, but I can't stop it." This is when I knew we had established trust, a bond in some way. I hugged him so hard that day! I loved him. It was on that day that Rubin and I made a plan that would last the rest of the school year. When he "felt it coming on," he would go and lie down in the art supply closet, where I had a pillow and a blanket on the floor waiting for him. And he would come out when he felt better. There was no interruption, no more screaming, just eye contact and a nod from his teacher. He became empowered. He began to feel like he belonged.

In the many days that followed, during nap time (yes, that's when five-year-olds were allowed to take developmentally appropriate naps during school), Rubin and I would sit in the hallway in my rocking chair and just rock, sometimes talked, but mostly rocked.

He would lie back on my chest and I could feel his body begin to relax, ever so slightly. According to the guidance counselor, his diagnosis as a "fetal alcohol and crack cocaine baby" meant he had a difficult time relaxing and sitting still. There was so much stillness in those moments.

Our talks in that rocking chair allowed me to learn so much about him. At seven years old (he had already been retained in kindergarten the year before I arrived), he was the oldest of four children. He would take his mom's food stamps and get on the bus to the neighborhood corner store to get bread, cereal, milk, and cheese for his siblings and bring it back home. I couldn't believe this was the same kid who couldn't recognize his written name. So we talked about how he did it, what he memorized, how he figured it out. Partly, it was his sense of belonging in the neighborhood. The city bus driver knew and took care of Rubin; the owner of the store in the neighborhood knew what Rubin needed and made sure he got the correct change back. The power of belonging in action.

I decided to make Rubin and his experiences the center of my unit of study called "Our Neighborhood." For one of the social studies lessons, I blew up a city map and as a class we traced Rubin's route from home to the bus stop, around the neighborhood, and back home. He was able to tell us about how he knew which bus to get on, how his neighbors helped, and how he helped his siblings. I can still see the pride on his face while he was teaching his peers (who, by the way, were sitting on the carpet with their mouths wide open in complete disbelief). I smiled so hard watching Rubin teach. That afternoon at the end of the day, as Rubin was running out of the room when his bus was called, he turned around, ran back to me, gave me the biggest hug, and said, "I can't wait to learn my letters tomorrow." That was the start of Rubin's journey to academic language that year. He felt confident and capable. It wasn't always roses, and we had many days of struggle, but Rubin's growth that year was one of my most rewarding experiences as an educator.

I bring this story up in this chapter because it demonstrates the deep need for belonging and the power of radical love. I loved Rubin in a radical way. I saw the goodness in him when no one else would take the time to do it. There was no special skill that was learned during my schooling, and certainly no quick-fix curriculum program. It was just me as a human connecting to him as a human. Building trust. Building community. It was seeing the good in his circumstances, in his experiences, in his spirit. This gift of seeing Rubin is always there. It's in all of us. We just have to be willing to do the work to find and nurture it for ourselves and for others around us.

PARENTING FOR BELONGING

All children need to belong. When they don't feel this sense of belonging, it impacts the way they see themselves and their place in the world. Right now, 7.1 percent of children between the ages of three and seventeen (approximately 4.4 million in the United States) have diagnosed anxiety disorders, and 3.2 percent (approximately 1.9 million) have been diagnosed with depression.[*] And that's just the ones who have received a diagnosis. And here's the surprising thing—the majority of these anxious and depressed children come from privileged, middle-class to upper-class families. Two of them are mine.

In her provocative book *The Price of Privilege*, clinical psychologist Madeline Levine describes that the new "at-risk" group of children is actually made up of preteens and teenagers of affluent families.

---

[*] Centers for Disease Control and Prevention, Children's Mental Health, "Data and Statistics on Children's Mental Health," https://www.cdc.gov/childrens mentalhealth/data.html.

These children participate in a variety of extracurricular activities, play sports and musical instruments, they have great grades . . . and yet, all of this is covering up what many of them are actually missing: a sense of belonging and connection. According to Levine, these preteens and teens are experiencing a higher rate of depression, anxiety, and overall unhappiness than any other group of preteens and teens in the country. These children often express feelings of conditional love based on their achievements and not on who they really are. My daughter has expressed her need to please her father and me. She's our oldest child, our only daughter, and our expectations for her were high. We positioned ourselves financially to give her opportunities that we thought would broaden her experiences and passions. It wasn't until she was heading off to college that we became aware that it was all too much. She knew she was loved. She knew she belonged and there was nothing that we wouldn't do for her, but she still felt pressure to be perfect, and in this perception she felt less connected. Perhaps it was the sacrifices we made. Perhaps it was the daily overscheduled agenda. She felt the pressures of being good at everything and the need to not make mistakes. And it came at a price.

From the outside, it looks like these children have all they could ever want or need. They have nice homes, money for vacations, presents at holidays and birthdays, parents who attend PTA meetings and volunteer at school fundraisers. What's missing? As parents, we want so badly to give our children the opportunities we never had. My parents certainly felt this way, as evidenced by the move from my old neighborhood. I, too, share that desire to do more for my children. But the trouble is that oftentimes we are so focused on what we want for our children that we don't take the time to hear what *they* want. Maybe they don't want to learn the violin or to play soccer. Our desires for them are so loud that our children have trouble finding their own voices, which can manifest as loneliness, anxiety, and depression now and when they are adults.

My daughter and I have gone to therapy together and separately. I am thankful that she and I have always had a relationship where we could talk about most things, and, looking back, I can see how we, as her parents, wanting so much for her, caused harm we never meant to. She saw our hopes and dreams for her as a need to be perfect, to be able to do it all. I can hear myself saying things like, "It'll help you get into a good college if you take these AP courses; do this extracurricular and your application will stand out; participate in this team sport or play this instrument, it's good for you and makes you well rounded." I wanted—and still want—my children to have choices in life, choices that going to a good college and having experiences can give them. The dilemma was that I was allowing my wishes, choices, and knowledge of a system that is rife with inequities—racism, sexism, and biases—to drown out her ability to actually make those choices for herself.

When this happens, kids stop feeling like they belong. They feel like they aren't enough, even when they're at home. They stop feeling like they have agency. In order to become a successful adult, someone who can work to make the world better, children have to have a core foundation of belonging, of acceptance, so that they can feel comfortable speaking with their own voice.

My husband and I had hard conversations about our children when they pushed back against all of the "wonderful opportunities" that we were making available to them. My husband didn't want them to give up any of the million sports that they were playing and I really wanted him to listen and honor what they were saying to him. "Dad, I don't want to play soccer anymore. I only want to play basketball," or "I don't want to play recreational ball anymore, I only want to do the travel season," or "I don't want to take piano lessons anymore, I don't really enjoy it." (Well, that piano choice was harder on me and hubby had to talk me off the ledge on that one.) My husband and I played many sports during our childhood and we wanted (honestly, we expected) our children would, too. We thought they would be excited about those same experiences. And for the most part, they really were. They love sports and we love watching them play, cheering them and their teammates on. Okay, the cheering on, loudly in the bleachers or the sideline, I have to admit, is mostly me. I am *that* mom, the loud one, cheering for everybody's children like they are my own—because somewhere deep inside, you know I think they all are. I've had moms on the other team ask me, "Now which one is yours?" I would reply, while pointing, "I gave birth to that one, but all of them [while waving my finger at the entire team on the field or court] are mine."

We want the best for our children, and aren't we as parents in the position to always know what the "best" is? NOPE! This feeling of thinking we know what's best for them is perfectly natural. Of course we sometimes have trouble distinguishing their identities from our own. This is where patience and grace are important—for our children and definitely for ourselves. We need to both know and accept who they truly are to create a sacred space of belonging in our homes, ones that say, "I see you, I know you, you belong here, you matter here." Sometimes this is where you lean into that grace—hard—in order to parent each child according to their specific needs.

PARENTING THE CHILDREN WE HAVE

With intention and care, we can create a space of belonging for our children, and the first step is to *know* our children. You have to begin by parenting the child you actually have rather than the child you wanted or the child you thought you would have. Let's face it—there are things about our children that we either don't want or are struggling to accept. I saw evidence of this often as a classroom teacher. Parents would not want to see that their child may have needed special services or would benefit from being in one of the group sessions with the guidance counselor. Or the parent is so sure the child wants to be on a team or take a course while the child is literally saying, "No, I don't want to do that."

Sometimes it's easier to love your children than other times. When you hear the idea of loving the child that you have, the way they need to be loved, it sounds obvious, right? I'm sure some of you are thinking, "Of course I do!" And yet, in the hustle and bustle of our daily, overscheduled lives, it can be challenging to think about the details of each child's individuality. The reality is that they are *not* the same, and each child has different requirements. It's important to set aside time for one-on-one dates with each of your children. It's how you get to know them, who they are outside the family dynamic. Otherwise, we tend to lump our children together—I know I have my own ways of thinking about how I refer to my kids, my "big kids" (the oldest two) and the three youngest are affectionately called "the boys."

My third child, Tyler, was the person who taught me this lesson in a very concrete way. Tyler is such a wonderfully unique soul. He has expanded my thinking and my capacity to actively listen and engage. He is my only child who is not interested in sports. We tried to tell him how great sports are and how much he would love them if he kept trying. He knew what he loved and we couldn't (or, to be more accurate, we wouldn't) hear him. Once I began to ask myself those hard questions—Is this about you or him? Are you showing up for Tyler? Where is your radical love?—I began to listen more and suggest less. In doing so, I got to know my son and he got to show me who he really is. He is the kid who knows everything about animals (especially reptiles), the environment, nature, anything science-related. He loves fishing and Beyblades and Pokémon and Anime. Oh my! Most of this was totally out of my lane. I had to lean back on radical love. How do I show up for him in a way that supports who he is and helps him know he belongs in a house full of sports enthusiasts? Let me tell you, I'm learning all sorts of new things. I've even become the grandma of a leopard gecko named Nuru, Swahili for "light." Although I am still learning the language of Anime and Pokémon, I am so happy watching him being happy and knowing that he is supported and radically loved.

Getting to know your children, outside your own desires and biases, can take some work, particularly if you haven't gotten off to the best start. It requires active listening, and encouraging your kids to do what *they* like, and participating in those activities with them. Tempting as it is, we can't force our children to always do what *we* enjoy. This also applies to what we think is right for them—whether that's academics, friends, or hobbies. We are older and know more than they do, and so we assume we know the right things for our kids. But we might not, and we need to listen when they tell us what's right for them. Family meetings are a monthly event in our house—it's how we make sure we're all listening to each other. Everyone brings a topic, and everyone votes on it or gives their perspective. I've got five kids, so we need a talking stick to make sure every voice is heard, but we manage!

In his book *Permission to Feel*, Marc Brackett, PhD, founding director of the Yale Center for Emotional Intelligence and professor in the Child Study Center at Yale University, suggests we must allow our children to feel and express their own feelings, unfiltered by our interpretations or guesses. But it can sometimes be hard for children to express their feelings and needs. My oldest son didn't like to talk about his feelings when he was young, so we kept a journal together. I would write something for him in our shared journal and leave it for him in his top drawer. When he was ready to respond, or when he had something he wanted to tell me, he would write something and put the journal in my drawer. This was how we were able to communicate; it gave him a safe space for him to express himself and it allowed me to stay present in his life. It's how I learned that his high anxiety was a form of OCD. He was able to tell me what he was experiencing through his written words. He would write poetry that provided snapshots into his thinking. The first comment the therapist said to me was, "You are so lucky he told you. Most boys his age never feel comfortable saying anything about their feelings and often turn to drugs, alcohol, and negative behaviors to cope. Good job, Mom!" Those words landed hard on my stomach. My mind went to the little blue journal that was in my top dresser drawer. Safe spaces. Open hearts. Consistent communication. Be as creative as you need to be to make it happen.

CREATING BELONGING

Establishing specific routines and rhythms in your home can turn it into a place where there is predictability, safety, nurturing, and belonging. Every family has to create its own cadence of security, one that makes sense for each member of the household. I can't emphasize this enough—it's so important to keep the needs of each individual family member in mind when establishing rules and routines for the household. It's not about having a series of individual rules and routines but, instead, a common ground that works for everyone.

For example, my husband is not a planner. He can pack at the last minute, he's okay with booking a vacation a week out from the day we leave. He's the dad who often adds another practice or training session to a kid's schedule the day of and calls me from work to let me know he can't get home in time so I, who am in the middle of cooking dinner, need to take said kid to the add-on training. And that kind of schedule has always worked well for him in his life.

My oldest son needs time to plan and process—and so do I! This caused many uncomfortable conversations and heated debates in our house over the years. But through trial and error and compromise, we have found routines and rhythms that work for our family. My son is not obligated to do additional training or last-minute sessions if they are too stressful for him. We have to give him at least twenty-four hours' notice. As far as vacationing, we still decide a week or two in advance, but our routine and rhythm is to alternate the types of vacations every year (one year a big city, the next year an outdoors nature trip). That at least gives me some control over knowing what to pack!

Routines and rhythms are about creating a home environment where your children know what is expected and where they fit in. Children often fear the unknown, but routines and rhythms bring comfort and consistency, creating a calmer household. This includes schedules, family culture, mealtime, chores, activities, community engagement, and so on. These well-established practices lead to confident children. Now don't get me wrong, it's not a cure to the organized chaos in my household of seven, but because we know what is expected, stress and anxiety are reduced (definitely not eliminated, but reduced). Not only does this help with family flow, but it also builds independence and confidence. My son Ryan is the keeper of the family calendar. He is diligent about looking at it every evening to inform all of us what our day will look like the next day—who's in charge of driving which child to practice, who needs to be picked up when and where. Not only does it empower his organizational skills, it keeps his mama on track (nothing better than an unpaid personal assistant in the house).

One of the most important facets of this household rhythm is a clear set of rules of engagement for the family, including how we talk to each other (one of my pet peeves is my children responding to my questions with "What?" or "Huh?"—oh no . . . Mama don't play that!), everyone having a voice (we use a Native American talking stick—otherwise there are just too many people trying to talk at the same time, making for a very loud house), not letting situations escalate before finding resolutions (I've been known to put two of my children in the same T-shirt for an extended time until they figured out how to get along, or made all of my children sit in a circle holding hands until they worked things out—amazing to watch how they figure things out pretty quickly).

I am passionate about being vulnerable with my children—it allows me to connect with them deeply and meaningfully. I know this may not be comfortable for every parent, but in your vulnerability, you are demonstrating courage and strength and giving your children permission to be their authentic selves. When my daughter Alexandra and I discussed her feelings of overwhelm and the pressure to be perfect, I immediately apologized and asked her for forgiveness. As a belonging advocate, how could I have missed this with my own daughter? I had to come to terms with the truth that there was a time in her life that my daughter didn't feel connected. It was shattering, but my heart remained open, to hear her and love her and to do better. I let Alexandra know that her experiences were real because they were hers.

Our stories and experiences dictate how we see and navigate the world. When creating routines and rhythms that align with a space of belonging, start with openheartedness, engaged listening, and making others feel like they matter. In her book *All About Love*, bell hooks reminds us that "a generous heart is always open, always ready to receive our going and coming. In the midst of such love we need never fear abandonment. This is the most precious gift true love offers—the experience of knowing we always belong." In order to create these routines and rhythms, you must start with having a clear vision for your family, as a unit.

WHAT'S YOUR WHY?

In his book *Start with Why*, Simon Sinek talks about the importance of knowing your Why. Although his work focuses on leadership in business spaces, I have adapted these main principles as a starting place for my mothering. As mamas, we are essentially the CEOs of our families. Sinek tells us that by looking at the bigger picture, we can shape our behaviors to drive long-term results. If you are reading this book, I believe we have a common long-term goal: raising children who are compassionate and socially engaged. Your "Why" is your purpose. It's what makes you get out of bed and work hard every day for your family. It drives you and supports the legacy that you want to leave for your children.

Families who have a sense of purpose become laser-focused on their goals. This doesn't mean the journey is always comfortable or that you won't have hills to climb and obstacles to get over—but knowing your Why will help you get back up when you fall, when you get off track, and when your children are going through a crisis. When my children were diagnosed with varying neurological exceptionalities, they were major blows to my family. We had to find ways to reset and move forward, altering and reestablishing a new "normal" each time. Our compass was and continues to be our core values. We know we can always return to these when we need to find a new path to our final destination. The clearer you are on this, the more you will engage in intentional behaviors, actions, and practices daily to reach your long-term goal: raising children who radiate joy and care genuinely for others.

I would like to spend a few minutes supporting you in creating your Why statement. Let's start by listing your core values. Your Why statement is carved out of these core values. In my house, we have five core values. They are the centering beliefs for my family, the foundation for my Why and the legacy that I want to leave to my children. Here are the Baxley House Principles:

1. **You are your brother's/sister's keeper.** This rule builds a sense of *belonging* and fosters *community* in the family. It's about teaching and modeling trust and interdependence. My children know that they are to put each other first (before friends) at all costs.

2. **Always give back.** There is such a general sense of entitlement in the world today. I want my children to know we have a lot, which means that we have the opportunity to give a lot. This rule teaches *compassion* (thinking of others) and *kindness* (recognizing our privilege and doing something about it) and makes social justice engagement a part of their lives.

3. **Own your own junk.** This rule is about seeing *perspective* and taking ownership and *responsibility*. My children aren't allowed to complain about what someone else did to them until they look at the situation from the other person's perspective first.

4. **Implement the Platinum Rule.** We all know the Golden Rule: Treat others the way you want to be treated. The Platinum Rule is about treating people the way THEY want to be treated. This

perspective requires *active listening*, *building connections*, and having *genuine relationships* with each other.

5. **Give joy/get joy.** *Being a light* for others is so important. But it's also important to be open to being the vessel for someone else's light. Be intentional about spreading positive light in the world. When someone wants to do something beautiful for you, receive that. It will bless you and it will bless the giver.

JOURNAL WRITING

Take a few minutes to write your core values for your family. I would even suggest that you do this with your children. This will allow them to have a chance to build these values and have a voice in something important to your family. Come up with three to five centering beliefs that are vital to who you want your children to become.

_____

_____

_____

_____

Once you've settled on your core values, see if you can come up with a Why statement that represents your parenting philosophy and the legacy that you want to leave for your children. Your Why statement should be simple, clear, actionable, focused on how you'll treat others, and communicated in positive language that resonates and aligns with your family's core values.

Here's my Why: *We consciously create and nurture a safe space in our home where compassion and kindness can take root, which grows our capacity for greater social impact in the world.*

JOURNAL WRITING

Create your Why statement grounded in your family's core values.

_____

_____

_____

_____

CHAPTER 3

RAISING ANTI-RACIST CHILDREN

When I dare to be powerful, to use my strength in
the service of my vision, then it becomes less and less
important whether I am afraid.

–Audre Lorde

Before I had kids, I joined an eight-week boot camp fitness class
with a friend. The group of fifteen of us met twice a day, six days a
week, and after spending up to four hours a day together for eight
weeks, we got to know each other well. I grew to love everyone in
the group, including our instructor, an ex-marine who punished us
each day with demanding but effective routines. During that time
he invited the whole class to his house for happy hours and din-
ners. It was an awesome bonding experience and we became like a
family.

As we were finishing up our last class with a long post-workout
stretch, teary eyes, and what seemed like an unbreakable bond with

our fellow classmates, our instructor, whom I genuinely loved at this point, asked his two children to pick up all of the equipment while we were stretching. His daughter, probably around ten, jumped right up and began picking the cones and the jump ropes. She turned around to her brother, maybe about eight years old, who was moving slowly, dragging his flip-flops across the basketball court, head down, shoulder slumped, and she said . . . wait . . . ready for it . . . "Stop being lazy like a nigger and help me."

I know your mouth just dropped . . . so did mine. My girlfriend and I—the only Black people present—looked at each other with horror. We were stunned—we did *not* see that coming. As we emerged from our fog of shock and hurt, we felt the eyes of the entire class on us. Nobody said a word. Not one word.

I had spent hundreds of hours with this group. I felt connected to them in so many ways. And yet nobody stood up for me. I'm not saying my classmates were racist. And I'm sure they would all describe themselves as "good" people, including our instructor. But in that moment, being surrounded by good people wasn't enough. Were they all ascribing this value judgment to Black people? Did they all feel this way? Probably not. I'm sure each of them would say, "I'm not a racist." They can even say, "I have Black friends," for my friend and I checked that box for them.

The thing is, simply being "not racist" is not enough. As Ibram X. Kendi said in his book *How to Be an Antiracist*, "The opposite of 'racist' isn't 'not racist.' It's 'antiracist.'" That's what my friend and I needed at that moment: the allyship of anti-racist friends.

The recent resurgence of the Black Lives Matter movement, in response to the killings of George Floyd, Ahmaud Arbery, Breonna Taylor, Rayshard Brooks, and too many others, has put the issue of racism front and center on our television screens and in our social media feeds. While racism has long been a problem in this country, recent headlines have served as a wake-up call for many parents, spe-cifically white parents. As a society and a culture, we are slowly ac-knowledging the effects of systemic racism. Many white people want to do the work of anti-racism, and many white parents know they have to do a better job of educating themselves and their children. Moms of color, particularly Black moms, want to know what more they can do to keep their children safe.

There are many social justice topics and issues that could be cov-ered in this book. But racism is the elephant in the room. We know it's there and we know it's important to deal with, yet it is often ig-nored, talked around, or politely sidestepped. We pretend it doesn't exist, particularly in spaces where there are many different types of people. I want us to move past that discomfort and really start dig-ging into *why* we think it's so difficult to talk about race. If we un-pack that, we can begin to have important dialogues with each other and with our children.

Racism is a reality of the world our kids live in—and it affects them, whether their parents talk about it or not. There is no magic wand to wave, no foolproof way of discussing the complexities of race, no single conversation that will resolve the issue for any family. The conversation is ongoing and it may be messy at times. And while it's never too late, the goal is to start talking about it when our kids are young. Others may disagree, but I truly don't believe it's ever too early to have challenging conversations, including those about race and racism.

We will almost certainly make mistakes here, and I may not have all the answers that you need—but I have my lived experiences as a Black woman, a Black mother, and a Black educator. And I can tell you that the reality is, you're probably going to say the wrong thing at some point. You're probably going to say or do something insensitive. The process of becoming racially aware means that you're starting in a place of being *unaware*. When mistakes happen, reflect, apologize if needed, be kind to yourself, and reaffirm to yourself that you're committed to learning. Do better next time, and keep trying until you make your next mistake, and then learn from that. This is the process of unpacking racism, and it's not going to happen overnight, and you're not going to be perfect at it.

You're going to be uncomfortable, but there's too much at stake to not walk through that fear. Just like most new adventures or encounters in your life, there is a (sometimes steep) learning curve. We teach our children the importance of follow-through and not to give up when things get difficult. Anti-racist work requires a commitment to never give up, a commitment of continuous action when things feel new and hard. We must model this process of struggle and continued effort for our kids. That's the journey to anti-racism. *Learn something new. Acknowledge the fear. Move through the discomfort. Take action. Repeat.* The more you put yourself out there, the more you learn to live in that discomfort, the more it becomes part of the process.

This reckoning can no longer be denied. This elephant in the room can no longer be ignored. Let's start the conversations that help us move beyond fear. In order to begin the work I want you to start reflecting on these questions:

- Why are we, as a society, so afraid of talking about race?
- Where did these messages come from?
- How are you passing these messages on to your children (overtly, covertly, consciously, or unconsciously)?

I want you to read the remainder of this chapter with the understanding that you are in a safe space for us to have real talk. We're going to acknowledge and name the fears, and learn how to move past them so that we can raise a generation of anti-racist kids. In order to get there, you have to examine your own experiences and be willing to listen and take responsibility for your role in changing minds and hearts—possibly starting with your own.

WHAT IS ANTI-RACISM?

The term "anti-racist" has roots in the abolitionist movement, in that it wasn't enough just to not own slaves—in order to be a decent human being, you had to fight against slavery as an institution. Anti-racism is the practice of actively working to eliminate the unfair treatment of people based on the color of their skin. It is making a commitment to dismantling laws, policies, attitudes, behaviors, and practices that are unjust and inequitable. The goal is to *actively* combat racism, not to simply be complacent in your own position of belief in equity. Action, no matter how small, is the foundation of anti-racist work.

Everyone has experience with racism. This isn't anything to be defensive about, or embarrassed about, it's just reality, and it comes from the world we live in. Beverly Tatum, psychologist, race identity expert, and author of *Why Are All the Black Kids Sitting Together in the Cafeteria?*, says racism is like smog in the air. You're breathing it in whether you know it or not, because it's everywhere and because it has become a normalized way of being in our society.

Reflecting on your own role in perpetuating racism is part of being anti-racist. Those of us who see parenting, particularly mothering, as a form of activism, must realize that if we are silent and do not resist the racism of our society, then we are complicit. We are passively maintaining the systems of power and oppression in society. Anti-racist work requires questioning, deep critical thinking, and intentional parenting. It requires doing what you know is best for your children, while also acting in support of the well-being of other people's children. This may mean engaging in difficult dialogue with family members and friends. It may mean standing alone in your choices or being unpopular with certain people or groups. Changing the world really does begin with the actions we take inside our houses. It has to start with the decisions, choices, and practices we're faced with every day. There is no checklist that you can tick off and then say, "I'm done." The work of anti-racism, and raising anti-racist kids, involves an ongoing, daily practice of modeling and interacting with your children and making sometimes difficult, conscious choices.

But before we start making those choices, let's begin by reflecting on your starting place, and the unspoken beliefs and biases that are often taken for granted.

UNPACKING AND ACKNOWLEDGING PRIVILEGE

The word "privilege" is frequently used in mainstream media, and we are often told to "check our privilege." To some, it can feel like an attack; others are simply confused about what privilege means and how it relates to them, still others think the term is meant for other people. So let's start with a definition. In the context of anti-racism work, "privilege" is defined as any unearned benefit, opportunity, or advantage given to someone because of their identity. Each and every one of us is privileged in one way or another. Because of race, a white woman is privileged where a Black man is not, and because of gender, a Black man is privileged where a white woman is not. When I ask you to reflect on your privilege, I'm not pointing any fingers or assigning any kind of blame—I'm simply asking you to observe your existing positions in society.

It is important for me to make clear that I do not assign a negative value or judgment to privilege. I don't want you (and definitely not your children) to feel ashamed if you recognize that you are privileged. The process of uncovering or making evident the ways in which we do and do not have privilege is simply a way to unpack the many layers of our identities—and the intricacies of the very notion of "privilege." In order to become allies in the cause of anti-racism and support people who are different from you, it's important to see the world from someone else's perspective.

It is not only necessary to unpack and discuss privilege and power with our children, it is foundational. Anti-racist children understand the impact of privilege on their lives and on the lives of others. Now, I know this is not the most comfortable task. I recognize it's complex and layered. Privilege is often weaponized in conversations about race in the media, used as a way to provoke guilt, anger, and defensiveness—which ultimately divides us further from one another. I want to offer a different way of examining privilege, one where we can accept it as a reality and leverage it as a tool for change.

In order to start to think critically and honestly about privilege, let's start with a journal writing prompt. This exercise is a way to begin the process that we will continue throughout the book—and one that you will continue for the rest of your life. We're never done learning, after all, and thinking critically about your understanding of your privilege is the first step toward changing patterns of negative (or neutral) practices in our homes and, ultimately, dismantling systemic inequality.

Journal writing: Take a moment to think about conversations your parents had with you about race when you were a child. I am talking about direct dialogue, eye-to-eye interaction. Write down what you remember.

When I ask people of color to do this exercise, they always have something to write. Actually they usually write fervently. When I ask Black parents these questions, I normally have to stop them from writing because there's so much to say. When I pose this question to white parents, the paper is often blank. Or I see words like: "No one talked about it" or "None" or "Not one, that's the problem." The fact that your parents never had to talk to you about race—*that's* white privilege.

Before you start to sweat, let's break this down a bit. Remember, we all carry privilege and we all have areas in which we're marginalized. The fact that in your house you never had to talk about race is one example of white privilege, but having white privilege is just one of the many ways that we do or don't have privilege. I want us to move away from using white privilege as a weapon. Instead, let's look at it as a tool for developing the awareness that creates change.

Peggy McIntosh, a professor in women's studies at Wellesley College and founder of the National SEED Project, is most famous for her article "White Privilege: Unpacking the Invisible Knapsack," where she created a list of the daily effects of white privilege in her life that she experiences exclusively based on the color of her skin. She calls it an invisible, weightless knapsack that's full of "special provisions, maps, passports, codebooks, visas, clothes, tools, and blank checks" that allows her to navigate in the world differently than her Black female colleagues. If, like Dr. McIntosh, you can honestly investigate your own white privilege, you have an opportunity to acknowledge your responsibility to serve and empathize with other people. This perspective helps us increase understanding and recognize how each of us can play an integral part in improving the inequities and injustices that exist in our communities or in society.

As an example, let me tell you a little bit about my identities and how they impact the way I show up in the world. As a Black woman, I feel very marginalized in our society, but there are also some areas where I know that I have privilege, and I can use those areas of privilege as a tool for change to serve those who don't have that same privilege. Specifically, I grew up in a household that was upper middle class. We never had financial issues, so I don't know what it means to struggle in that way. I want to use my privilege to support underserved communities, so I work with children in spaces where there is socioeconomic struggle. I work hard to be an ally and support families in need of resources I can provide.

Another example of my privilege is that I am heterosexual and cisgender. I can use that privilege to support the LGBTQ+ community. I have some leverage because of my academic status, and I have used that privilege to support my doctoral students and their work published in higher education on issues faced by the LGBTQ+ community.

Just because we benefit from one kind of privilege doesn't mean that we benefit from all kinds of privilege. Similarly, what may bring us benefits in one situation may at other times result in our having less power than in other situations. For example, as a mother of five children, I am often asked by other mothers for my opinion and support because of my wide experiences raising a large family with very different needs. In these spaces, my choice to have a big family is an asset and affords me a kind of privilege. However, I've also been advised throughout my career not to reveal how many children I have because some would view me as unserious about my research. My motherhood in this case is seen as a deficit or pathology to being a dedicated scholar. When you're reflecting on your experiences and your childhood memories, it's important that you look deeply into various aspects of your life and how you've embraced or rejected notions around identity, privilege, and power.

Let's dig a bit deeper into the identities that you hold. The following table offers a way to assess your privilege by ranking the privilege afforded to you by your various identities. As you read through each category, identify whether your identity within that space is traditionally privileged or traditionally marginalized. Mark "P" for "privileged" and "M" for "marginalized." After you've completed the chart, I want you to study your intersectionalities—categories where you have multiple points of privilege and where you have multiple points of marginalization. You have to be open and honest in your reflection, for it is only with reflection that we are able to be intentional as we move forward into anti-racism and Social Justice Parenting.

There may be some gray areas that you encounter as you reflect on your identities, for example, if you are of mixed race or ethnicity. I would ask you to think about the way you navigate in the world with those different categories of identity. How do you self-identify? Another approach is to think about how you perceive the way people see you. You have to decide what makes sense in the way that you show up in your life and the lives of those around you. When you fill out your list, also think about these questions:

- How was your childhood impacted by these identities?
- In what ways have these identities clouded the lens you use to see the world?
- How do these identities play a part in the way you raise your children?

Again, privilege is not negative, it's just a way of being. The process of uncovering or making evident the ways in which we do and do not have privilege is a way to unpack both the intricacy of the notion and the many layers of our identities.

"P" OR "M"	IDENTITIES	PRIVILEGED*	MARGINALIZED*
	Gender	Men	Women, transperson/gender
	Race	White	People of color
	Class	Middle and upper class	Poor and working class
	Nation	United States or "First World"	"Second, Third Worlds"
	Ethnicity	European	All others
	Sexual orientation or gender identity	Heterosexual or cisgender	Lesbian, gay, bisexual, or transgender
	Religion	Christian	All other religions
	Physical ability	Able-bodied	Persons with disabilities
	Age	Youth	Elderly persons
	Language	English	All other languages
	Brain differences	Neurotypical	Neurodivergent

*The identities are labeled as privileged or marginalized based on the current power structure in the United States.

ACKNOWLEDGING COLOR, ACKNOWLEDGING RACE

I know I made it crystal clear that the message of this book is in-clusive of all the ways in which people are marginalized, but I really have to save this space to address the well-meaning white people (sorry, not sorry . . . I said I was going to be honest here. We're friends, right?) who are so excited to be a part of the movement but don't really do their homework on race relations first. Please, please, I'm begging you, from this day forward, do not ever say that you don't see color! It's simply not the truth. You can't *not* see color. *Everybody does!* Babies as young as six months old can notice racial differences, and children between the ages of two and four start internalizing race-based biases. And just so you know, every person of color *knows* you see color. After all, they see color, too, and the mere fact that you mention color in your claim that you don't see color belies your statement. Take a moment to reflect: When do you make this claim? If you or your children are spending time with other white people, do you say "I don't see color" to them? Or do you only not see color when you're with people of color?

I recall going to a women's mindfulness retreat where, at the end of the session, we were asked to say something about our experience. I said I wanted to thank the women in the circle for opening their hearts and spirits to me and how I'm always hesitant about going into these kinds of spaces as a Black woman, and I wanted to honor their openness. After the session was over, another participant, a white woman, said to me, "It's so nice to meet you. Thank you for coming. Honestly, I never saw your color until you said that. I just didn't notice."

Really? Just like I didn't notice her red hair? Of course I did. She has red hair. I have brown skin. These are facts. I had to bite my tongue to stop myself from pointing out the disingenuous nature of her comment. I just smiled and said, "Really? That's interesting," and walked away. But I walk around in my Black body every day and feel the weight of everyone seeing my color. Acknowledge that for me. Validate my experiences of racism and marginalization so we can work on moving past it.

The next month when I went back to the women's circle I politely pulled aside the woman who didn't see color and said, "I've been thinking about what you said about not seeing my Blackness. I know you thought that was loving and inclusive. But it was offensive, and let me tell you why." We went on to have a candid and constructive conversation, and she and I remain friends to this day, years later. If I had not taken the opportunity to engage in a dialogue with her, she likely would have kept "not seeing color" and offended others in the future.

Was it my "job" to do that? No. A lot of people of color are exhausted by the burden of constantly having to educate white people on their racist behavior or explaining the impact of microaggressions on their mental health. I get it. I get tired and overwhelmed, too, and sometimes I need time to recharge or recover. But most of the time, I choose to put in the effort, because I want to make a difference. I want my children to live in a world where their worth is not entangled with society's complex relationship with race. It's a big part of why I wrote this book and why I am sharing my thoughts with you.

When people of color are told that you don't see us as a person of color, it's as though you're telling us that you don't see our experiences of discrimination and systemic racism. You're not doing anything to help me—you're only comforting yourself. You're making *yourself* feel like a good person. In fact, in downplaying the reality of race, you're further silencing and marginalizing people like me. And to take it one step further, you're teaching your children that it's inappropriate to talk about race, which continues the cycle of ignoring people who are different from you. Remember the elephant in the room? He's sitting on my chest.

Think back to your childhood. How did you learn that it's right to say or believe that you don't see color? Maybe it was overtly discussed, or maybe you received this message covertly. Now think about what message you're sending (overtly or covertly) to your own children. I know this type of reflection can be challenging, but it's essential to building our practice of Social Justice Parenting. You have to do the work! Social Justice Parenting is about changing our practices for the next generation to create a passion for closing the privilege gap. How we help our children in the development of these practices (and attitudes) sets a foundation for radical love to take hold.

Remember, racism is like smog, and your children are breathing it in, no matter what you do. There's no way for you to filter it out entirely. Instead of trying to deny its existence, teach them how to see what is too often invisible, so that they can work to clear the air, making it safe for everyone to breathe. Talk to your children about the concept of privilege, about how differences in privilege make circumstances more difficult for some groups of people, and use real-life examples. Often when young children ask questions about physical differences in public (e.g., "Why is he missing a leg?" or "Why is she so small?"), parents become embarrassed and are quick to "shush" their child or change the subject. They feel the need to put out the fire by suffocating the flame. But your child's curiosity is worth addressing. And if the subject of the question is within earshot, he or she is less likely to be offended by a child's innocent question than by a parent's disinterest in teaching a child about diversity. You can address questions like these in a direct yet sensitive way. Recently, one of my friends, who is white, texted me about something her seven-year-old daughter, Leslie, said in the car. This was our exchange:

Friend: "Today when we were in the car driving home, Leslie was describing the girls that she was playing with earlier in the day. Is it wrong when she describes one girl as 'brown'?"

Me: "No, it's not wrong. Brown is the color of the girl she was playing with. Leslie is using it simply as a description. She is being honest about seeing color. It's refreshing and it's the right thing to do."

By addressing your children's questions or comments in the moment, you demonstrate your strong support for others, and your willingness to not take part in the further marginalization of another human, even when it's uncomfortable. You make the choice to flex your parenting activist muscles. The only way to raise children who can dismantle racism is to identify it, talk about it, and push back against it. Yes, it can be challenging, but deciding to start the journey and push back against the strong pull to create an invisible bubble of protection around your children is the first step. Each action that you take will have rippling effects on the lives of your children (and mine).

"THE TALK" IN BLACK HOMES

For Black families, there is another, more painful ritual that is performed at an early age. "The Talk" is a time for Black families to educate their children about their cultural identity and to prepare them to face racism, discrimination, and stereotypes in the world. It is a way of covering our children with psychological armor, helping them survive outside the safety of our homes. As Black parents, we are constantly fighting against the generational trauma that we have endured throughout the past centuries. This cycle continues to repeat itself, with no true solution for healing. Every time we read about another senseless death in the paper or see more trauma on the television, it triggers all of those feelings that systemic and structural racism bring. I often get asked by well-meaning white people why these conversations need to reference slavery. "Why do we still have to talk about slavery? It happened so long ago," they say. My answer: Because its legacy still lives on within the bodies and experiences of Black people. In her TED Talk, Brittney Cooper, cultural theorist and author of *Eloquent Rage*, captures this idea well. She says, "Our memories are longer than our lifetime." I'm talking about generational trauma, not just in remembering what happened to our ancestors but also in the downstream impacts of slavery, like incarceration rates, educational disparity, income disparity, maternal mortality rates—the list goes on and on. Systemic racism impacts our mental health, resulting in decreased hope, feelings of disconnectedness, increased risk of depression, a sense of invisibility, and despair. Triggered trauma, like seeing another Black man gunned down by law enforcement, wakes feelings of powerlessness, mistrust, and anxiety, and we relive our ancestral trauma over and over. These cycles remain constant and will stay that way until systemic racism is dismantled.

"The Talk" is a Black parent's way of equipping our children with rules and directives for how to cope with this legacy and with a society that was built upon inequality. It's an oral manual that has been passed down for generations, with instructions on how to thrive in a world that's not always kind to you. Every time another killing of an unarmed Black person is in the news, Black parents are sitting with their children to review the list of dos and don'ts that are needed to stay safe. Don't resist the police. Keep your hands visible at all times and be as still as possible. Don't run. Don't wear that hoodie. Don't put your hands in your pocket. Don't speak until you've been spoken to. Do tell them your mom works at the university. Do tell them your dad is an attorney. Do tell them where you live (which is in a predominantly white community—and when I say predominantly, I mean everybody except me and my kids). Do be polite. Do exactly what they say. Writing this list brings tears to my eyes. What a burden for Black children to carry. And contrary to what some may think, it's not only our boys who have to sit down for "The Talk." Young Black girls are having their own talks. They are perceived as older and less innocent because of the color of their skin. The process of adultification for Black girls can begin as young as five years old. A study by the Georgetown Law Center on Poverty and Inequality showed that adults view Black girls as less innocent and more adult-like than their white peers, especially in the age range of five to fourteen. The results of the survey also revealed that these same adults believe Black girls need less nurturing and less protecting and to be supported and comforted less than white girls. And further results showed that there is a perception that Black girls are more independent, know more about adult topics, and know more about sex. These stereotypes lead to Black girls disproportionately receiving punitive treatment in schools and within the juvenile justice system.

Black mothers have to try to balance protecting their daughters and allowing them to fly. We tell them to speak their minds but not too loudly. We tell them to own and connect with their emotions but not to let it come off as angry. Imagine having to censor your daughter because the world doesn't like her hair or skin or her "attitude" or her confidence.

What a burden that any Black child has to carry in a world that is covered with the smog of the generalized racism felt by those around us, and the systemic racism of built-in inequalities of work, education, incarceration, maternal mortality rates, police shootings, and so much more. This is the lived experiences of Black moms, and it doesn't go away when the headlines fade and the protesters have gone home. It's not a load that we can pick up and put down when we get tired or weary. It is a heavy permanent cloak that we wear every day. There's no keeping our children in the protective bubble. There's no way of practicing color blindness when the world reminds you every day that you are Black. There's no letting fear silence us into not talking about racism and other hard topics. As Black mamas, we don't get to live in that space. We don't get to choose because the world has chosen for us.

If you stand up and do the work as an anti-racist, you can lessen that load on families all over the country. Not only can you stand in solidarity and actively denounce racist behavior, both individually and systemically, but you can raise children who see the value of all lives and who will work to dismantle white supremacy as they grow up.

ALLYSHIP

On that last day of boot camp, I was looking for allyship, for someone to stand with me and for me in that moment. Allyship is the act of decentering yourself in order to make space for others who are different from you, those who are, at that moment, marginalized. It is an intentional act of humanizing the experiences of someone other than yourself and using your power and unearned privileges to act with and for others in pursuit of ending oppression and racism and creating equity. Allyship is an action: a consistent and arduous practice of unlearning and relearning and consciously putting the needs of others first. Conversations with your children about racism, oppression, and inequities are important and needed, but if we are trying to create permanent change, allyship is the broader message that parents need to instill in their children.

Allies have long been a crucial component of social movements in our society. White allies have stood beside Black activists, from slavery abolitionists to the civil rights movement to today's Black Lives Matter movement. You and your children can be a part of something bigger than yourselves, something critical in the historical narrative of our society. Talk to your child about joining the long and rich line of allies who have worked to effect change. Talk about how your allyship can be even more effective together as a family of anti-racists.

One of my clients, who has such an open and honest heart, wanted to be more active in her ally work but kept hitting roadblocks. She talked with me about how she had experienced trauma in the form of a sexual assault and often brought up this experience when working with the Black community. Her intention was to find a way of connecting, of saying "See, I can relate to trauma." This didn't work well for her, and she wanted to understand why. I explained that true allyship doesn't happen that way. If you are going to be of support to others, you should not expect those people to be in a space where they have to hear your trauma, even if your intention is to find common ground. It's not about common ground—common ground involves *you*. You don't have to be an ally to relate to the people you are serving; in making yourself an ally, you have centered yourself and your trauma in a conversation that should be entirely about them and their trauma.

I would also advise would-be allies to do as much learning as you can, but not to then move into *teaching* people of color. Your knowledge is never greater than their lived experiences. Honoring and respecting their lived experiences requires you to listen more and talk less. You don't have to fully understand what oppression feels like to be an ally. Being an ally means taking on the struggles and battles of others as your own. Being an ally means standing in unconditional solidarity to the people and the cause, without seeking their validation for the work that you are doing. You should never be in front, and you should never take charge unless you are directly asked to do so. You are transferring the benefits of your privilege to those who lack it in that moment.

Allyship helps you move from protecting your children to teaching your children how to protect and stand with others. Going back to my opening story, my fellow boot camp participants chose the role of bystander. Did they say terrible things to me or actively participate in the racist incident? No, they didn't—but that wasn't enough. We have to teach our children that being a bystander ("not racist") results in the same damage to the offended party and perpetuates the same inequalities that gave rise to the hurtful statement. Those women had an opportunity to tell our instructor's children that the N-word was offensive. They had an opportunity to show them what it looks like to be an ally. Instead, it was just another situation where Black women stood alone. We were the ones to denounce the value judgment, push back on the word choice (both the racist slur and the historical narrative of calling Black people lazy), and acknowledge the crude way of thinking (that ascribing a negative value or attribute to all people within a group was essentially narrow-minded, in this case racist). It should not have been ours alone to do. In that moment, we needed allies.

Teach your children how to be upstanders instead of bystanders. Offer examples of other young people who have made a difference as allies. I think about the young people of all backgrounds who took part in the national Black Lives Matter protests. I also think back to the students of Stoneman Douglas High School, who shared the national stage with survivors of gun violence in Chicago, in Washington, DC, and in South Los Angeles. Those children's stories and experiences would have never been heard otherwise. The Parkland students used their power and privilege to make sure the world heard the voices of children who face gun violence on a daily basis. These are real-life examples of allyship in action that are appropriate for kids of all ages.

Being an ally is an ongoing process that requires courage and compassion. You will make mistakes, just as you would with any other new skill. Our words and thoughts are shaped by systemic oppression and racism, and when engaging in ally work, there will be times when you have to confront implicit biases and other internalized notions that are found in your unconscious psyche. You may catch yourself clutching your purse a little more tightly when a Black man is walking toward you. Notice that it happened and recognize where it came from. Other times, someone may point out to you when you've made an assumption about someone based on their race or when you've made a thoughtless comment. A white friend of mine was joking with me about how her young daughter was "slaving away" in the kitchen. The words had no impact on her, but they did on me, and I had to let her know. She was embarrassed and apologized, and we moved on. When these issues are brought to your attention, be open to receiving and accepting the criticism with humility and grace. "I apologize. Thank you for letting me know."

Don't get stuck in the mistake. Apologize. Fix it. Move on. Keep working.

It's important to note that in the work of allyship, you may lose the friendship or support of some people who are currently in your life. There are going to be people who do not like watching you moving in the direction of an ally and anti-racist, as they feel it threatens their own protected status or privilege. You may be confronted by family members, friends, or even coworkers or other parents in your community. If this work is important to you, you have to be aware that these things may happen, but you can't let them stop you.

STARTING SOMEWHERE

If this seems like a lot to take in, let me tell you that it's okay to start with small steps. You don't have to drop everything and become a civil rights lawyer or become an overnight expert in anti-racism. The key to moving in the direction of being an anti-racist is intentional, conscious action. Let's start right now. Take out your phone. Seriously, take it out and click on your contacts. Begin by conducting an informal inventory of the people you know. How would their identities look if they were to complete the table from this chapter? Are they mirror images of your identities? For those contacts that *don't* look like you, think about the context of your relationship. Is this a client or coworker? Is it your housekeeper or nanny? Continue with a series of inventories on various groups of people in your life, like your neighbors, your place of worship, where your children go to school, and any other groups that you are around on a semi-regular basis. Reflect on the messages that this may send to your children (without you saying a word). Beginning the journey of anti-racism starts with simple changes that add up to bigger changes. If you can't diversify the people on your phone, you won't be able to tackle the systemic issues in our country. There's always some action that can be taken. Think about starting with these:

- Unpack your own childhood experiences with race and privilege.
- Intentionally let go of biased ways of thinking.
- Believe and value the lived experiences of Black people. (This is a challenge even for some Black people, due to internalized oppression.)
- Normalize "Blackness" in your daily routine.
- Make it a point for your children to see Black and Brown professionals (doctor, dentist, pharmacist, tutor, music teacher, etc.).
- Model what it looks like to take action against racism.

Okay, now go to your children's rooms. Look in every toy box and on every bookshelf and examine the movies/videos on their electronic devices with a critical eye. What messages are your children receiving about your family's values about diversity? Is the physical environment inside your home set up for your journey with anti-racism? You can start by making sure the things your children are playing with and learning from represent a spectrum of identities, ideas, and experiences. A little diversity—even in something as simple as toys or books—can be a start in exposing your child to the differences in people's lives.

These simple exercises won't change the systemic racism that my children experience in society, but it is a step moving you into anti-racist work with your children. Mind you, these small actions are not substitutes for hard conversations with your kids. There is no escaping that. If you want to start with reading a book with your children to open that door, you know I am a huge proponent of the power of children's literature. If you want to start using the terms "fair" and "not fair" with your children, I'm okay with that, too. The key is to get started, but the minute you feel comfortable with what you are doing, move on to something that scares you. These are simply entry points into a more conscious state of awareness for you and your family. You no longer can keep your children in that bubble and do nothing more than sit around feeling sad that there's racism and inequity around you.

Things may not always work out. You won't always say the right thing. But we can't live in that space of fear. We can't parent effectively in fear. Honor yourself in that space of radical love and do things that scare you. This doesn't mean you should jump into situations blindly. You want to make sure you do your own homework; don't always look for someone to do it for you. You will need support filling in the gaps of your anti-racist journey—after all, you don't know what you don't know—but you can seek out those answers for yourself, starting with actively listening to the voices and lived experiences of Black people. Carol Cox, the host of the podcast *Speaking Your Brand*, challenged her listeners during Women's History Month to listen to only women-hosted podcasters, read books that were written only by women, and watch news programs that were anchored by women. It was a pretty empowering exercise. What if you took that same approach to studying the lives of Black voices and learning about Black lived experiences? Soaking in the Black experiences through listening, reading, and watching will help shift the way you think about your own unconscious biases and judgment about Black people, helping you undo unconscious value judgments about who and what you think Black people are. And then, as you become aware, use that newfound awareness to address gaps in your children's understanding and answer their curious thoughts and questions.

Are you thinking that you want to start anti-racist work with your children but you aren't sure what to say? Here are some conversation starters that can open the door to dialogue, leading to more anti-racist behaviors and practices in your home.

NAMING RACE (INCLUDING YOUR OWN)

- "Do you see the children's different shades of skin in this story? The lighter skin, like ours, is called white. Look at your skin. It's not really white, it's really peach. When children have skin that's darker shades, like this character, it's called black. It's not really black, right? I love seeing all of these different color skins. They are all beautiful."
- If your child notices and comments on the color of someone's skin: "Hmmm, you're right. That's a great observation. It's nice to see different kinds of people/skin."

- "Look at your skin and your hair. Your friend's [Black friend] skin and hair are different. I love how beautiful and different they are. How are they different to you?"
- "Have you ever noticed if there are different race/ethnic characters in the books that you read? When you read a chapter book and you have to imagine what the character looks like, do you ever imagine it's a character of color?"

EQUITY (FAIRNESS AND UNFAIRNESS)

- "A racist is someone who is mean to another person based on the color of their skin. See your skin? People call that white skin. Other people have different/darker skin color and they are treated differently because of it. In our house, we want to learn ways that we can work to end racism."

  Slavery was when people with black skin had to work without getting paid and were treated badly by people with white skin. That means people with white skin owned them and people with black skin didn't have any rights or freedoms. And because of this history, people with black skin are still treated unfairly.
- "Racism still exists. I see it when Black people are not getting paid the same amount of money for doing the exact job as a white person. I see it when people call Black people names because of the color of their skin. Do you see it at your school? What can we do about it?"
- "Police officers are supposed to 'serve and protect' people. Most of them do a great job at helping us. But sometimes police officers hurt people, and the people that they hurt are often Black people. That isn't fair or right."
- "We are white and we don't really have to worry that a police officer might hurt us. In Black communities, many people are afraid of the police officers because of the history of being unfairly treated."

- "Black and brown people have been treated unfairly for a long time in this country, and they still are. Some people think because your skin color is different that you don't deserve to have all the things that white people have. We don't believe that in our house."
- "There are a lot of people who are sad and angry because a police officer hurt a man because he was Black. What do you think about that?"

CONFRONTING STEREOTYPES

- "You know sometimes we have assumptions about people based on their race or their gender. Do you ever do that? Let me tell you about a time that I did and how I reminded myself to be mindful of that."
- "I don't like this movie/video/show. It's making fun of people. It makes me [add your feelings here] because people shouldn't be made fun of because of [add your descriptor here]. How does that make you feel?"
- "There are a lot of people in the world whose lives and experiences are very different from ours. Let's learn about other people's lived experiences and try to understand these differences."
- "If we only read books about white characters or only watch videos with white characters, our understanding of the world leaves out a lot of what helps us understand why there are injustices in the world and the more we learn, the more we can see what makes the world so wonderful."
- "Many white people didn't want Black people to live near them or go to the same schools with their children, so they wouldn't sell houses to them in certain areas of town. How do you feel about our neighborhood and who seems to fit in and who doesn't? Why do you think that is?"

ANTI-RACISM/ACTIVISM
(CHILDREN AS CHANGE AGENTS)

- "Sometimes we have to speak up when things aren't fair, even when it's hard. It's okay to tell me you are scared. I get scared, too."
- "When white people speak up and work with people of color to change laws that aren't fair, it makes the world better for everyone."
- "When you stand up for and work with a group of people who are different from you and you want the world to be better for them, you are called an ally."
- "An ally is like a good friend who always makes sure you're treated fairly and is always on your side."
- "An activist is someone who sees something that is unfair and decides to do something to make it better. How can our family be activists?"
- "What if someone told you that you couldn't do something because of the color of your skin? How would that make you feel? What could we do to change their minds?"
- "People are protesting because they think something is unfair and they want it to change."

PART II

LAYERING THE BUILDING BLOCKS

CHAPTER 4

REFLECTION

While no single aspect of Social Justice Parenting is more important than any other, Reflection comes first in my ROCKS program because before we can engage in the practice of raising a generation of socially conscious kids, we must do some soul-searching.

We can't expect the world to change until we reflect on, examine, and resolve old ways and old wounds. You may feel tempted to skip over this part, because it's not easy and we don't always like what we find—but it is essential. If we aren't honest about how our experiences have shaped our thoughts and actions, we cannot intentionally engage in the work of raising more empathetic and compassionate children. As a mom, I recognize that I must equip my children with the tools to liberate themselves from ignorance and oppressive practices in order to embrace and enact a pedagogy of hope and love in their own lives. That starts with my own accountability, including taking stock of the experiences of my childhood and their impact on how I show up as a parent and as a human being.

WHAT IS SELF-REFLECTION?

In order to make a deeper change, you have to look more closely at *yourself.* Who are you? What words would you use to describe yourself to others? Let's take a moment and do that right now. Describe yourself in five sentences.

Did you find that exercise easy? Or did you struggle a little? Did you think about what you thought other people would have said about you? Or were you able to use only the qualities that you see in yourself? I know when I first did this, it was difficult not to define myself by external factors (what others have said about me, the work that I do, my various roles, etc.). But if we want to show up as our authentic selves or get serious about changing those parts of us that may not align with who we want to be, we have to know who we are when no one else is around. Who are you when there are no expectations from others? Who are you at the core of your being?

Self-reflection is a practice that nurtures and enhances our understanding of who we are, how we became who we are, and why we think and act in the ways that we do. It is a deliberate habit of spending time with your thoughts, feelings, emotions, and behaviors and questioning what you do and why you do it. It gives you a clearer picture of yourself and your values and how to align those truths with the way you *want to* parent and show up in the world. It is also a gift to your body and your brain, giving you a chance to take a break from the chaos, the noise, and the stress of your daily life. It allows you to focus on how you can support the people who matter the most in your life (please make sure you are included on that short list).

One night my eleven-year-old came out of his bedroom crying after being in his bed for only five minutes. It was already later than his normal bedtime because I allowed him to stay awake to watch the end of the NBA playoff game (Go Heat!). It was also nearing my own bedtime after a long day of work and household chores, so I was feeling the weight of the day creeping up on me. I asked him what was wrong (and not in my warmest, most caring voice). He said his hand hurt. To offer context, each of my children is responsible for cooking dinner one day a week, and this had been his night to cook. Earlier that evening, he reached to move the handle of the pan and burned his hand. He had been icing it all night. During the game, my entire family was screaming and jumping and laughing, cheering our team to victory—my little guy included! So when he came out of his room crying, well, let's just say that my level of empathy was a little on the empty side. I gave him more ice, burn ointment, and ibuprofen and sent him back to bed. Five minutes later, he came back crying again. I questioned the timing of his hand hurting and sent him back to bed.

As I sat on the couch, exhausted, I went into my self-reflection mode. Once I connected my actions (not really hearing my son), my feelings (being too exhausted to connect with him), and his feelings (he was hurting and not being heard), I changed my course of action. I got myself off the couch, sat right next to him in his bed, and held that baggie of ice on his hand, rubbing his forehead with my other hand. I said, "I apologize for not hearing you. I know your hand hurts. I was just tired and impatient. Thank you for cooking dinner. I am here until you fall asleep." Fifteen minutes later, he was asleep. He needed me, and my moment of self-reflection helped me be there for him.

Reflecting on our behavior and our thoughts allows us to see what we need to work on. You can't really know yourself if you don't spend intentional time thinking about what makes you react the way you do and what triggers those reactions. As important as it is to pay attention to your actions in the past, it is even more helpful to be able to use self-reflection in the present, allowing you to respond to situations instead of reacting to them, and then having to undo something you've said or done that may have been hurtful to the people you care about. Self-reflection can serve as a guide to taking a deep dive into your thoughts and motivations and can support you in feeling less lost and more empowered in your parenting.

Reflection allows you to examine various facets of your life, as an imperfect being, parent, and community member. It allows you to shine a light on those areas that you want to work on, areas in which you are successfully serving others, and ways that support your growth in caring for yourself. Practicing self-reflection takes discipline and intentionality. It requires honest self-talk and authentic assessment. We can sometimes create a made-up persona without really knowing how we got there. When we engage in honest reflection, we force ourselves to remove the filters and ruminate on our true, genuine, vulnerable selves with curiosity and care. This can be hard work, but over time our increased self-awareness will enable us to move away from fear and lean into radical love.

Now, if you're anything like me, you might spend your mornings trying to quickly blend a smoothie or gulp down a cup of tea or coffee while making sure the kids are up/getting dressed/eating breakfast/ brushing their teeth. And then you're packing lunches, making sure they have all their things together for school/soccer/dance class, getting out the door in time to get one kid to the bus stop before heading to the car drop-off circle before the line gets too long and you're late for work—and that's when everything is running smoothly! With mornings like this, who has time for reflection? It's easy to get caught up in the daily grind of our lives and use our busy-ness as an excuse for not being present in the moment. We operate from a zone of autopilot and often miss the benefits and joys—as well as the difficulties—of what we're experiencing. How can we learn and grow from our experiences if we don't take a minute to reflect on them?

I encourage you to find a few moments for yourself each day when you can pause, take a deep breath, and reflect on the day. These stolen moments can completely alter the way you show up in your life. This momentary pause in your busy schedule (and your busy mind) will help you build a life that is meaningful to you, your family, and your community. This practice has helped me to make sense of the way I respond to situations in my business, with my husband, and with my children. It's allowed me to see the ways that I can be better and ways that I can respond (instead of reacting) when situations don't go according to plan.

Let's work through a 3-2-1 reflection activity together.

JOURNAL WRITING:

1. List three (3) things you do well in your daily parenting that bring you and your child(ren) joy.

_____

_____

_____

My example: (1) Open dialogue and family discussions; (2) bedtime reading to younger kids (I want this to last forever—I will even volunteer to read one of my older kids' textbooks with them just to snuggle and read together); and (3) family dinner time.

2. List two (2) things that you do as a parent that you want to change.

_____

_____

_____

My example: (1) Yell from room to room to get the kids' attention instead of getting up and asking them face-to-face; and (2) Not listening as closely to my children as I would like to when they need my attention while I'm working.

3. Pick one (1) of these items (the most pressing at this time) from
   your "I want to change" list that you want to address first.

_____

_____

_____

My example: I notice when I'm working and my children come to talk to me, I can get impatient or I tell them I'm too busy to talk right now. I often forget to circle back around to ask them what they wanted to talk about. I am afraid this is not reinforcing my ideas of belonging. I don't want the children to feel like what they say is not important. If I'm not listening to the small stories, why would they come to me when they have big issues and situations?

4. First be aware of what is happening. Then think about what triggers this reaction or action.

_____

_____

_____

If I tune in and pay attention to my behavior in the moment, I find myself half listening while they are telling me something, or I get impatient if they take too long to tell a story and I tell them to hurry and finish their thoughts for them. It happens most often when I'm working—deadlines are particularly triggering. If I'm in the middle of a thought, I worry that I will lose the flow of being creative or productive. Or (and this is where I get vulnerable and honest with you) sometimes it's just that I think my kid's story is going to be about a subject that I have no interest in or knowledge of.

5. Create an action plan for how you will work on this.

_____

_____

_____

I go back to my base: radical love and my family's core values. I ask myself: Am I practicing the Platinum Rule? Am I treating my son the way he wants to be treated? Are my actions rooted in radical love? I created a "Need to Talk" whiteboard close to my desk. When my kids want to talk while I'm working, they'll write what they want to talk about on the board. This system allows me to focus on my work and allows them to know that what they have to say is important and worth documenting for me. When I'm done working, I follow up with each of them.

6. In this situation, what does "reacting" look like? What would "responding" look like, instead?

_____

_____

_____

Reacting looks like sounding exasperated or putting my finger up to tell them to wait. It also looks like my children acting impatient or frustrated when I can't talk right away. Responding would look like my giving them the thumbs-up or a smile when they are writing on the board. Responding also looks like quality time with my kiddos, going through our whiteboard list during a time when we all feel relaxed and attentive.

They are my hell yeah, every time. Big picture: They are learning patience and I am able to get work complete and enjoy more quality time with each of them.

REFLECTING ON CHILDHOOD

We all grew up with certain ideas or beliefs that have stayed with us, consciously or unconsciously, throughout our lives. In addition, the ways our parents responded to our needs, feelings, and concerns had a profound impact on us. We are shaped by our childhoods. We know this—it's why we try so hard to be good parents to our kids. But if we aren't aware of the ways our childhood continues to influence us, we can unwittingly perpetuate it, passing our experiences and beliefs down to our children. And so one of the first and most important steps in the work of self-reflection is to reflect on your childhood. What were your parents like? What were their values and what were their expectations of you?

I mentioned my dad in an earlier chapter and his experiences during Jim Crow and the civil rights movement. These interactions and relationships created a mistrust and parenting fear for his children in the world. He often tried to shield us from racism by calling on us to keep our guard up and not get too close to white people. But he and my mother knew how important it was to expose my sisters and me to opportunities that would open more doors for us as we entered the world as adults. My mother always encouraged us to follow our hearts, keep our feet on the ground, and remain open to possibilities. She was more trusting and was vocal about the importance to finding good people to bring into our lives, no matter their backgrounds. I believe this was the foundation of my passion for belonging. It became important to me that I surrounded myself with diverse people, and today I want that for my children as well.

In one of my workshops, I met a young mother named Diana. In her reflection work with me, she recalled how neat her house was growing up. Her mother collected china, and they lived in a fairly ritzy suburb where everything had to be just so—the lawn had to be trimmed, the sidewalks had to be swept, and inside, everything had to be put away in its proper place. Diana's home, like those of most parents of small children, was mostly filled with toys and generally a mess, and she worked hard to be fine with that. But she had noticed that when her toddler spilled a drink, even just a cup of water, she would feel a sense of panic. She would rush to clean it up and demand that her son be more careful. It was obviously an overreaction, and she couldn't seem to control it. As she reflected on her childhood, she realized that this panic response must have come from her own upbringing, when spilling a cup of water was a big deal, and she needed to bring awareness to her actions so she didn't pass them on to her son.

Like me, Diana is working on rewriting the scripts of her childhood that no longer serve her and actively integrating those wonderful traditions and memories that support her values and goals. For instance, Diana grew up going to Cape Cod every summer. It was a time when she could explore the shoreline, chasing crabs and biking to the arcade and watching movies at the drive-in. This was an experience and tradition that she wanted to make sure she carried on with her own children—and she did. Today, her kids enjoy the same kinds of carefree summers. And while some traditions have changed—traffic on the Cape limits bike riding—others, like exploring the shoreline and catching crabs, remain the same.

This is not only an experience but a value. Creating spaces of belonging and the importance of family were values that were modeled for me growing up. Time spent in nature, time spent just with family away from work and stress—those are values Diana wanted pass along to her children. Our values are reflected in what we *do*, and that is truly what we are accessing when we practice self-reflection. What are we *doing*? What are we proving to ourselves and others about our values? It's about being mindful of your actions and their impact on others.

Take a few moments to consider your childhood and the memories that stand out, both positive and negative.

JOURNAL WRITING

Write down two memories from your childhood, one positive and one negative. Then reflect on how these experiences have shaped the kind of parent you are today.

_____

_____

_____

_____

We learn how to parent from our parents. Sometimes we intentionally choose the traditions and values we want to repeat; sometimes we repeat patterns from our childhood without realizing it. Conscious reflection helps us decipher the impulses behind our habits. For instance, if your mom was always a very cautious person, and never let you run around or climb trees or go for a bike ride by yourself, you too might be overly cautious with your kids; or you might overcompensate by being overly lax. Either way, you're unlikely to become aware of the motivation behind your behavior if you don't reflect on your childhood as well as your current behavior. Being thoughtful about where your instincts come from and how your childhood influences your parenting allows you to be intentional about what you choose to keep and what you choose to improve upon. After reflecting on your childhood, you may realize that you felt held back or sheltered by your mother's protectiveness. You can acknowledge that feeling and then make an informed decision about how to raise your children so that they feel free but are still safe.

Now, I recognize that this is easier said than done. If you're carrying trauma from your childhood, self-reflection can be both challenging and painful. Trauma lives in our bodies, like a force of energy that we can't see, but it impacts our lives until we get to some resolution. It's hard. I get it. But it's so important. If you're looking for a reason to do this difficult work of self-reflection, what can be more meaningful than your children?

THE REFLECTING CYCLE OF PARENTING

As parents, we have to continuously reflect on what our children see, hear, and feel from us. With the big ideas, the major topics in the world—like environmental justice, racial justice, and gender equality—I try to reflect on how I show up. I want to raise my children to understand and take on these issues as they become young adults . . . to do better than I have done in the past. I have made mistakes, and I can't set a good example for my children unless I face those mistakes. These are just a few of the ways I haven't always shown up as I would have wanted to:

- I didn't speak up when others needed me to speak up. *What am I doing to empower my children to self-advocate, to speak their truth, and to stand up for what's right?*
- I've internalized the falsehood of thinking that being a "good person" is enough. *How am I showing my children that being a "good person" requires them to be allies, activists, and agitators?*

- I've welcomed the momentary comfort of not being "othered." *How do I teach my children to be proud of who they are as unique human beings?*
- I've accepted society's narrow and limited narrative of certain groups of people. *How am I supplementing what the world teaches my children and how am I making sure the messages they receive are inclusive of all groups and that they reject stereotypes and limited beliefs?*

What am I teaching my children through my actions? This is the question I often ponder. Parenting is like being stripped down and looking in the mirror, seeing the best and worst of yourself. We're constantly modeling for our children, whether we think about it or not. Our kids take in and absorb everything we say and do. When they're younger, their imitation of us is cute and amusing, even flattering. When they become preteens, we may feel embarrassed when we see ourselves in their less desirable attitudes or behaviors. By the time they're teenagers, it becomes a battle as we try to get them to change long-engrained behaviors or beliefs.

As you begin to incorporate more self-reflection in your parenting, using the following REFLECT exercise can help you remain open and authentic to the process.

R—Reflect on your response. Have you ever said or done something that you regret the moment after you do it (emoji raised hand, right here)? Or wanted to say something but held your tongue because you were afraid of saying the wrong thing? I think this fear prevents many people from having conversations about race with their kids, other family members, and friends and colleagues. You have to identify the fear and name it before you can take steps to change it. This means slowing down and seeing what the situation calls for, as well as going into self-reflection mode. What external factors, internal factors, or past experiences influenced your reaction? Was there something not related to your child that caused you to react in a certain way? Was your response appropriate to the situation? From a social justice perspective, did you grow up in a household where people didn't speak about race-related topics? Did you grow up in a family who looked down on or who made racist remarks about groups of people? Were you able to voice your feelings, fears, and concerns? Was your house a safe space for curiosity and questions? All of these things matter. They make up your story. The more you can reflect on your childhood narrative, the better you can show up in the present, in your parenting. Children with parents who are effective at reflection grow up to be more secure and grounded and are better problem solvers. As they watch you self-reflect, they will learn from your example and become proficient at trying to show up as their best selves.

E—Evaluate how you were feeling. Name the feelings that were triggered (both positive and negative). Make sure there is an accurate alignment with what's coming out of your mouth and what you are really feeling inside. Many adults have a difficult time identifying feelings, and unfortunately we pass that disconnect on to our children. I know that my husband, like many men in our culture, has a hard time expressing hurt and fear. I've been with him for almost twenty-five years and have seen him cry four times total. When it feels like everything we taught our children is not sinking in (from table manners to missing curfew), my husband's go-to emotion is anger. What he's actually feeling is fear that they will go out into the world and make mistakes, get hurt, or they won't be ready. But what my kids hear is screaming. My feelings, as a Black mother, are often wrapped up in making sure they know how to conduct themselves when they are out of my sight based on their Black skin. I try—again, not always successfully—to balance a realistic awareness of racism and a healthy dose of concern about what's going on in the world. If we identify our true emotions, we can shift our behavior to match what we are actually feeling.

F—Find out how your response made your child feel. This is a critical stage of the REFLECT Cycle. Don't be afraid to ask your child how what you said or did made them feel. For example, when you have made the decision to talk about things that scare you and topics that speak to the injustices in the world, there's a need to go back to your children and follow up on how it's impacting them. You can begin teaching your children positive socio-emotional development, as it influences a child's self-confidence, capacity for empathy, and ability to meaningfully connect to others. Give them the tools and vocabulary to reflect on and identify deeper, more nuanced emotions and feelings. It starts with you being able to name your own. I highly recommend Marc Brackett's book *Permission to Feel*. Brackett says that feelings are a form of information. The way we think and behave impacts the way we feel, but we don't always know why or how to deal with those emotions. Understanding and articulating emotions are skills that we have to learn and teach our children.

L—Lean into your family's core values. Always let your core values and radical love center you. When you have gotten off track or your words or actions don't align with who you are or who you want to be, your core values are the navigational system, the GPS, that will get you back in alignment. Go back to the core values and the Why statement that you created in chapter 2. (If you skipped this activity, go back and complete it. We will continue to refer back to your core values throughout our time together.) If you are reading this book, I imagine your core values center around raising anti-racist and compassionate children. Your core values shape the culture of your home and are the essence of who you are and what you stand for. These core values should support your decision making, including what you say and how you show up for yourself and your family.

E—Explore additional ways you can respond/show up in the future. This is where you show your willingness to grow as a person and as a parent. We know we don't have all the answers. We also know that we have to change the tools in the toolbox often as our children grow and transform and as the world around us demands it. Don't be afraid to seek out support to navigate in spaces that you aren't familiar with. Get a coach (like me!), talk to other mothers with similarly aged kids, read books and educate yourself (thank you for choosing this one!), try individual or family therapy (I've done both!).

C—Capture a time for a little grace and to catch your breath. I'm going to say this again, just in case you missed or skipped it . . . there is no perfect parent. You are going to make mistakes, some small and some ginormous, especially on this journey of raising children who stand up for others. It's inevitable. So when it happens, look in the mirror and say, "Hi [insert your name]. Welcome to the humanness of parenthood. I am exactly where I need to be in my journey as a mother/father, remaining open to learning and growing. I give myself permission to be vulnerable and I accept myself and my child as we are." Find a moment of peace, sit in it, breathe through it, remember what it feels like. You will go back there often. I will meet you there.

T—Take action. Use these previous steps to guide your next actions in your Social Justice Parenting journey. Be mindful and present and continue to incorporate reflection in your daily routine. There is so much to learn about yourself and your children in the reflection.

LEAVING PERFECTION BEHIND

Here's a hard truth: None of us are error-free as parents—I'm certainly not! I'll make mistakes in the moment and not act according to my values (like when I was tired and didn't want to give my son some extra love the night he burned his hand). Or I'll put a lot of thought into a particular decision about my children, and I'll *think* it's right at the time . . . but soon realize my decision didn't serve my children but was self-serving.

When I decided to homeschool one of my sons, I felt very strongly that I was making the best decision for him. Traditional schooling wasn't working out for him or for me. I constantly had to go to the school and flex my "professor" muscles to advocate for his needs.

The first year was great. We unschooled for a month, and then spent a couple of months really diving into what ADHD was and what that meant for him. The rest of the curriculum was all about what Tyler loved; it was loaded with everything science (natural habitats, reptiles, experiments, dinosaurs), Black history, and his love for Egypt and Greek mythology. We visited museums and wetlands, and science experiment classes for homeschoolers. We took nature walks, worked outside, and joined a club to build a community garden. It was fantastic. Things were well planned yet flexible. Until the second year.

My most social and outgoing kid (honestly, he's never met a stranger he didn't like) was feeling lonely at home. He wanted to go back to a classroom setting with other students. I'm not going to lie: At first I felt a little disappointed that he wasn't loving what I had created for him. I mean, really, who wouldn't like a curriculum designed just for them, right? But once I pulled myself and my feelings out of the equation, I knew exactly why he needed a class. I know my son. He loves people. He loves his mama, for sure, but he needed to socialize with his peers. And so it was. All of my plans, and the hours spent on research, and the change in my schedule to accommodate his schooling . . . it all went away. I enrolled him in a small private school with other students like him. He's been there for four years now and he is well adjusted and happy.

It is not possible to achieve perfection. You *will* make big messes sometimes. And when that happens, lean into it! The road to Social Justice Parenting is a winding one, one that requires mistakes in order to grow. We tell our children that mistakes are how we learn, and that same truth applies to us. If we can learn from our mistakes, we can do better and parent with confidence—until we make the next mistake, and then learn from that one. When I talk to my children about controversial current events, I fumble trying to explain it in a way that they understand and in a manner that doesn't cause them more anxiety. I never avoid these conversations, but sometimes I don't have enough information, or I let my big feelings complicate or cloud my delivery. Just like anything else, the more we reflect on the process and continue to try to make it better, the more likely we are at getting the outcome that we want. Sometimes it's as simple as taking a deep breath, counting to ten, or stepping back from the situation for a moment. Whether we're talking to our children about social justice issues or just trying to get through our everyday routines, the centering of radical love should be the goal. Our own experiences often trigger the need to "get it right" and we inject that into our children.

I know a mom, Nikki, who is a crafter, but when she tries to do a project with her daughter, Maile, things never seem to go well. Whether it's painting or knitting or sewing, the activity always ends in frustration and/or tears. Often Maile will have a vision for the project that Nikki knows is impossible to achieve. She'll try to gently explain this to Maile, and Maile will suggest one impossible, illogical solution after another. Nikki, whose past experiences have made her a bit of a perfectionist, is triggered by her daughter's suggestions. Her desire for the project to be done correctly conflicts with her daughter's fanciful creativity, and without realizing it she goes to a place where her past issues come rising to the surface. This place is where our own fears and vulnerabilities live, and sometimes we aren't at our best in those moments. Nikki gets triggered when Maile insists on doing something more complicated because it makes her feel inadequate, like what she's offering isn't good enough. She gets frustrated by her inability to deliver on Maile's enthusiasm and takes that enthusiasm for a slight on what creativity she *is* able to offer.

I can relate to this with the work that I do. Do you think my kids want to attend every march or take up every cause that I think we should? When my children don't treat each other with compassion and kindness, I get triggered. But I also know that my kids are just being kids, trying to figure it all out.

So is Maile. She's just an imaginative, ambitious kid who always wants to try the hardest thing. I've suggested to Nikki that she try to understand the feelings that are brought up on both sides of the situation. The reality is, our kids sometimes want things that are impossible for us to give or don't behave in ways that align with the values we hold near and dear. This can bring up feelings of inadequacy. This doesn't feel good for anyone! But sometimes it's unavoidable. When that happens, let yourself feel those feelings— and let your child feel their disappointment. It's okay. You both get to have your feelings, and it's when we deny ourselves and our children that right to feel that we end up reacting in ways that we later regret.

By allowing herself to sit with her feelings of frustration and inadequacy, Nikki can stop limiting Maile's creativity and ambition.

She can actually listen and allow, and maybe they can try one of Maile's ideas. Maybe they won't work out (they probably won't) but so what? They can have fun and enjoy a day together, which was the whole point in the first place. Nikki is learning to let go of the perfection and frustration that comes from a place that has nothing to do with her daughter and to get back to being present and having fun.

THE POWER OF SELF-REFLECTION

As difficult as it may seem to reflect on our childhood experiences, our honest version of ourselves, and how we are parenting our children, the benefits make all this time and struggle more than worth it. For starters, self-reflection can help you gain perspective. It's easy to get lost in our own emotions and allow a tunnel vision of how we see the world to creep into our daily thinking. Reflection allows you to pause, step back, and focus on what's really important to you and your family. It's about taking a minute to shift your thinking from what's going on around you—kids pulling on your shirt telling you they're hungry, boss calling you about the deadline on the project, baby crying—to observe what's going on with you inside. This pause can support the next decision that you make—one that you won't regret and one that you can live with ten minutes and ten years from now. Self-reflection gets you back to the honest, real you more quickly.

There's another side benefit to doing this work. If you are able to move past your trauma, you may be able to reach a state of acceptance, even forgiveness. I know sometimes that word, "forgiveness," can be triggering, depending on the circumstances. I've had some issues with this word when I think about the circumstances that surround my mother and my biological father. For me, forgiveness is about choosing to let go, to release the power that the trauma has had in my life. It's about finding peace within and not allowing those feelings to block me from living my best life with my children. Again, it's not easy. Sometimes forgiveness isn't the ultimate goal. Sometimes it's releasing or shifting the power of the trauma. Everyone has a different level of trauma and a different way of dealing with it, so I don't want to make it seem like I'm asking you to do something that isn't right for you. But in my experience, self-reflection is the only way we can move past our traumas, so that we can parent with intention rather than reacting against our traumas or perpetuating them.

Getting through it will require you to sit with it, to process it, and to feel all the feels. It can be helpful to have someone that you can talk it through with, either your partner or a friend, but if you don't feel comfortable sharing, write it all down in your journal. I am a huge fan of unsent letters. This is a ritual of writing letters to the people who may have caused you pain in the past and, instead of sending the letter to the person, you burn the letter as a way of letting go and moving on. I will repeat an affirmation or read quotes while it's burning. Here are a few examples that may support your unsent letter ritual:

- "When I let go, I begin to find peace and grow."
- "I am enough. I am whole."
- "Forgiveness is the greatest gift you can give yourself."—Maya Angelou
- "We do not heal the past by dwelling there; we heal the past by living fully in the present."—Marianne Williamson
- "I am not what happened to me, I am what I choose to become." —Carl Jung
- "Forgiveness is giving up the hope that the past could have been any different."—Oprah Winfrey

Other practices that I think are helpful include visualizing the "letting go" process. Close your eyes and watch yourself releasing the energy from your body. Visualization can be a powerful tool to guide your mind to moving to a healthy place. Give yourself time and space. If you feel like this chapter is triggering past traumas for you and you feel overwhelmed, don't handle it alone. Visit a licensed therapist to support you in your journey of letting go and finding peace. Do the work to heal that little girl inside you. Listen to the teenager in you that was never heard or validated. Your present self and your children are counting on you to heal her.

Self-reflection helps us to live in our truth more deeply and more consciously. Often, as busy women and mothers, we simply react to whatever is going on around us. Showing up for yourself—putting on your oxygen mask first—so you can show up for others can't be done, with fidelity, until you take a look within. When we reflect, we are better able to consider the consequences of what we say and do. It helps us to think about how others may interpret what we say and how our actions may impact our loved ones in a negative way. Reflection can also challenge limiting beliefs and assumptions that may get in the way of your own growth and that of your children. This is a great time to reflect back on your parenting fears. How are these fears impacting the way you show up and respond to your children? How is there a misalignment with your core values and your parenting fears? How is this misalignment passing on childhood traumas for your children? Remember, reflection is ongoing, fluid, and continuous. It gets easier as it becomes a part of your routine. I try to reflect in the moment, before I open my mouth. Clearly that doesn't always work. What I am good at is reflecting at the end of the day to see if I showed up in radical love during various moments of the day. When my actions and words didn't align with my family's core values, I try to make it right.

Self-reflection supports our ability to learn, relearn, and unlearn. It empowers us to build emotional self-awareness through critical examination and questions, which can lead to self-improvement.

JOURNAL WRITING

Consider reflecting on the following questions and write your responses in your journal:

- What is the impact that I want to make in the world? The legacy that I want to leave for my children?

_____

_____

- What are my family's passions and how do we tap into them to serve others?

_____

_____

- What are my limiting beliefs—about myself, my partner, my parenting, my children, the world—and how do I work to overcome them?

_____

_____

- How are the people closest to me (family, extended family, friends, etc.) or the people I spend the most time with (could also include colleagues, team members, coworkers, etc.) impacting my life?

_____

_____

• What have I learned about myself over the last year that can help me to continue to grow into the person, mother, activist, human being that I want to become?

_____

_____

ESTABLISHING A SELF-REFLECTION PRACTICE

Your self-reflection practice can look very different from mine. Find something that rings true for you and makes sense with your lifestyle and your personality. Some people like to add this to their morning routine. In my crazy busy house, there isn't a lot of time to myself once the day begins, but even just getting up thirty minutes before my kids allows me a little time for quiet self-reflection.

Or you might find it easier to find time at the end of the day, right before bed. Honestly, I find myself reflecting during that time as well. You can use a journal to record your thoughts and to have the option to reflect on your written words at a later time. Another great time to engage in reflection is when you're out in nature, perhaps during a morning bike ride or walking the dog in the evening. The point is, just start having these conversations with yourself and allow yourself to reach your authentic, honest self so you can be the best version of you for your children and for our community. The world needs you!

CHAPTER 5

OPEN DIALOGUE

Honesty and openness is always the foundation of
insightful dialogue.

—bell hooks, *All About Love: New Visions*

I was sitting in the public library with my children one day after
school. I overheard a conversation between the mother and daughter
sitting at the table next to us. I'm guessing the daughter was about
seven or eight years old, and the conversation went like this:

Child: I think I want this video, Mom.

Mom: I don't know about that. It's kind of sad.

Child: How is it sad? It's about horses and I love horses.

Mom: It's sad because they aren't nice to this horse [pointing to
a horse on the cover]. Let's get something else.

Child: But I'm sure it has a happy ending, Mom. And I love
horses. I want to get it.

Mom: I know, but I don't want you to get that one because it's
sad. Find something else.

I watched the disappointment on the little girl's face as she slowly walked back to the shelf to replace the video box.

It's easy to find ourselves redirecting young children, telling them that we know best. You may hear yourself saying, "Because I said so!" or "I'm the parent!" Although this mom didn't directly say "I know what's best for you," her actions certainly gave her daughter that message. And the truth is, this isn't the message we want to be giving our children. We don't always know what's best for them, and if we don't listen to them, we never will. Social Justice Parenting requires maintaining an open dialogue with your child, which means you must take time to actively listen and validate your child's voice. I'm not saying the mom should have let her seven- or eight-year-old borrow *Pulp Fiction*, but if we don't give our children opportunities to practice using their voice at home, they won't know how to use it in the world.

AUTHENTIC OPEN DIALOGUE

As a professor in multicultural education, inclusion, and belonging, I teach the work of educator Paulo Freire, specifically his philosophy of critical pedagogy, which asks students to question—and, when appropriate, challenge—practices and ways of thinking that marginalize, specifically the ways that existing power structures reinforce patterns of inequality. I've also been able to integrate some aspects of Freire's work into my parenting. I'm drawn to his ideas around the championing of the oppressed, the importance of actively and open-heartedly listening to others' stories and experiences, and the need for mutual respect and love—as always, a deep, radical love that is unselfish and willing to struggle with and for others—when engaging in open dialogue. Authentic open dialogue involves speaking and listening with active hope, courage, and humility.

Active hope is not wishful thinking or positive affirmations. Active hope is something we do, an action we take when we're searching for ways to create more justice in the world. Hope is sometimes described as a passive activity—we sit around, "hoping" for change. But *active* hope means taking steps to achieve that change, even when we're in the midst of anger, despair, and sadness. It's easy to work for change when we feel good. It requires active hope to work for change when things are hard. And right now, things feel hard in the world.

Open dialogue requires us to have the courage to be vulnerable with our children and with ourselves, while checking our egos at the door. I show up with my children as I am, warts and all. As I continue to do that, my children gain the confidence to do the same. Sometimes that looks messy (fearful, frustrated, sad, angry), but in that moment, it is my truth. Being able to witness my imperfections and the way I work through them teaches my children that there's no "bad" or "wrong" way to feel, *and* that there are constructive ways of healing or moving through those feelings. That's a sacred lesson to teach and learn.

In open dialogue, everyone is given the space to tell their truth. It's not one person "depositing" their knowledge and ideas into another person. Instead it is an *exchange* of ideas, concerns, and energies. It fosters growth and change and allows us to understand each other's perspective and circumstances. It requires us to be open to our children's opinions and knowledge, and it asks that we allow them to be in the role of teacher.

That may sound odd to you. Parents are often assumed to be correct, and because of age and experience, sometimes we are. But if we let the power differential between parent and child get in the way of listening, we slowly drown out the voices of our children, and they become unable to use their voice out in the world. When practicing

Social Justice Parenting, we have to listen to and affirm our children's voices. It doesn't force one dominant, powerful voice but instead re-examines cultural assumptions that would have us silence or disregard a young person's voice. Children have important and valid perspectives, even if they're different from yours. Learning about their viewpoints will ultimately help you learn more about your child, and who doesn't want that, especially during puberty and the teenage years when they would rather walk on glass than talk to you every day about the issues they face? If you and your kids get used to talking together about the tough stuff from an early age, it'll be so much easier for them to talk to you about the things that really matter when they're older.

Children often ask questions that we, as parents, are not always comfortable with or prepared to answer. What you tell your children is important, but how you act during those discussions is crucial. Addressing hard topics actually can make your children feel safer. I know that sounds counterintuitive, but it gives them some control over the messaging that they are receiving, and it gives them a safe place to answer questions and unpack scary or unfamiliar topics.

When my oldest two children were around six and four years old, my mother-in-law was diagnosed with breast cancer. My husband and I wanted to tell our children right away. I got children's books to read with them as an entry point to the topic of cancer and then we had critical conversations with the kids about why Grammy may lose her hair, why she may not have the energy to swing them around like she normally does, and why she may be tired. We also discussed ways that we could help support her. My husband and I tried to answer the hard questions they asked, such as: Is Grammy going to die? Will you get cancer, too?

My sister-in-law made the decision that she didn't want to tell her children. They were the same ages as my children, but she felt that it would be too traumatic for them. While I totally respected her way of dealing with this major change in all of our lives, I had to prepare my own children about what to share and not share with their cousins, who didn't know anything about Grammy's cancer.

Everyone is going to make different choices about what is appropriate for their families, and you have to make the right choice for your family. You know your children best, and you know what they can handle. But one thing I'd suggest you consider is that when you're the one to initiate a dialogue about the hard things, you can manage how that conversation goes. As our children grow up, their peers and social media will have more influence over their understanding of these issues than you may, especially if they're not used to having weighty conversations with you.

I was out one evening walking with one of my neighbors and she said to me, "Traci, Zoe now knows about sex! I didn't think she really knew so I asked her what she knew and she told me. Guess who she learned it from?" Yep, you guessed it! My children are THOSE KIDS! When my daughter was about nine we'd already had the "sex and where babies come from" discussion. After the run-in with my neighbor, I had a follow-up talk with my daughter. "In our house there isn't anything that we can't talk about. I will always try my best to be open and honest, even when I don't know the answers, even when the questions and answers are hard. However, not every family shares these same house rules. So sometimes you can't tell your friends the answers to hard questions because their parents want to be able to tell them when they are ready." She seemed to understand what I was saying but walked off and said, "Mom, it's really not a big deal. Everyone should know." I smiled to myself, feeling pretty proud of her in that moment.

Troubling events will pop up on our kids' phones and flash on their computer screens, like the shooting of an unarmed Black citizen or an insurrection at the US Capitol catching their attention. Who do you want to explain these events to your kids? Who should give them the context to understand what is happening and process how they feel about it? Do you want to leave it up to your child's peers or media? In a Social Justice Home, we must use these opportunities as teachable (and learning) moments for the whole family.

NEVER TOO YOUNG

One of the most frequently asked questions I receive about the concept of open dialogue is, "What is the appropriate age to start talking about social justice issues or topics that are (fill in the blank here—hard, taboo, stressful, not happy, scary, etc.)?"

My answer is clear and consistent: Your children are never too young. Let me repeat that for all the moms who just tuned me out, who are ready to skip down a couple of paragraphs, and who are saying to themselves, "She doesn't know my child." Yes, Mama. I'm talking to you. Your child is not too young to have these conversations. I am going to engage you in a quick, easy-to-read, and crystal clear conversation (or perhaps you may consider it a monologue) about child development. I want you to really take this in. Remember, we're friends here. I've confided in you about my family's business, and you've promised to walk this journey with me in radical love. Give me your hand . . . let's get through this fear together.

Here's the deal: From the first year of their lives, babies begin to notice similarities and differences. There's research to support that they notice differences in emotional expression (happy versus sad faces) and differences in skin color as early as six months. By the age of two, children are using gendered language and have internalized some idea of gender. When my daughter was two, she would sit with her baby dolls and pretend to breastfeed each of them. Most children, including transgender and gender nonconforming kids, begin to identify with a specific gender around the age of three.

Our expressions of our children's genders often begin even before we take them home from the hospital—with caps and the onesies assigned by sex, baby clothes we've carefully selected, or our choice of nursery decor. We use language like "That's my big, brave boy" or "Come here, my sweet girl" when we talk to them. While these choices are innocent enough, in recent years it's become clear that over time enforcing such culturally imposed gender roles may severely limit our children, preventing them from fully exploring their identities.

Young children are continually making sense of the world around them, taking in and modifying their ideas along the way. It's important to be prepared for their inquisitive thinking. What messages do you want to send your kids? By the time they're preschoolers, ages three and four, they begin asking more specific questions about gender identity and physical attributes. "My hair looks like Mommy's." "Why is her skin brown?" "Why does he look like that?" We reinforce this with the clothes they wear and the activities we enroll them in (dance, soccer, cheer, basketball). You might hear comments from your child like, "He can't go to ballet because he is a boy," or "I don't want to wear pink, that's for girls." They begin to recognize different family structures and gender roles that are reinforced in your home, in school, and on television. Be proactive and think about your responses for questions like, "Why does she have two mommies?" or "Why is his daddy peach when his mommy's brown?" Kids this age also begin to develop a greater understanding of other people's feelings and needs. You'll hear questions like, "Why can't I have Air Jordans like Todd?" or "Why does that man sleep outside instead of in a house?"

By age five they show implicit racial attitudes and understand that certain groups hold higher status than others. Sadly, this is when you may hear sentiments like "I don't want my skin to be brown" or "I hate my curly hair!" When I was a kindergarten teacher, I taught a unit called "Community Heroes" where we learned about the people who made our community thrive. I showed my students a picture of a diverse group of people and asked them which one of the people in the picture is a doctor? Which one is a scientist? Which one is the bus driver? Which one is the nurse? Which one is the housekeeper? Almost every child chose the people of color as the bus driver or housekeeper.

At five years old, children are also curious about body parts. Again, previous kindergarten teacher here, I can assure you this is absolutely normal. (I've witnessed several private show-and-tell sessions comparing body parts!) Children at this age begin to create personal and social identities. They know what it feels like to belong and are clear on when they don't belong. Do you recall the story I shared earlier about my daughter feeling left out of a group because she wasn't Jewish? That incident took place in kindergarten! This is also the age when kids begin to internalize messages that are constantly being sent to them—overtly and covertly by you, by their siblings, classmates, teachers, media, and society—and form an identity based in part on these observations. "She's too shy to make friends." "He's wild, but boys will be boys." "She needs to be less bossy." "He's too soft; he better toughen up."

A great example of the impact of societal messages on the development of children's identities is the famous doll study conducted by African American psychologists Kenneth and Mamie Clark in 1947. In the study, the couple studied the preference of Black children, ages three to seven, for dolls with white skin. When the young children were asked to point to the doll that they would like to play with, that they liked the best, or that they thought was nice, a significant percentage of the children chose the white doll. When asked which doll was bad, the majority of the Black children pointed to the black doll. What I found most devastating about this study was that when the Black children were asked to identify the doll that looked most like them, some would start crying and run out of the room. This powerful research and the Clarks' testimony were instrumental in the court decision of the 1954 *Brown v. Board of Education* case where "separate but equal" was deemed unconstitutional.

These messages are also building blocks for the way children perceive other people and their awareness of social power based on various identities. Stereotypes, prejudices, attitudes, misinformation . . . all before their seventh birthday. Now you tell me, do you still think your child is too young to begin having open dialogue about topics he is already forming ideas and opinions about? What do you want your child's first understanding of race to be? What about socioeconomics and issues of poverty? What about gender identity or bias? Do you really want to leave the introduction of these topics up to the media and society or their peers?

If fear is preventing you from speaking to your kids about hard things, let me suggest a reframing of that fear. You should be more afraid of the messages your children are receiving out in the world, messages you are doing nothing to counteract if you continue to think they're too young to receive them.

THE FEAR IS REAL

We talked a lot about fear in chapter 1, but we're coming back to it now because frankly, fear is the single biggest obstacle standing in the way of radical love. In the case of open dialogue, I notice that the fear of discussing difficult topics has little to do with the child but rather is directly linked to the parent's own discomfort, whether that's due to past experiences or to anxiety that the conversation may take a turn in a direction that the parent is not prepared to go. Unfortunately, things do happen in the world that can have a huge impact on our children and on the way they see and navigate the world—the 9/11 attack in 2001, Hurricane Katrina in 2005, the Sandy Hook shooting in 2012, the Flint water crisis in 2014, the 2018 shooting at Stoneman Douglas High School, the 2020 global pandemic, the racial unrest in the summer of 2020 . . . the list goes on and on and on. Depending on the age of your children, these events happened in their lifetime. There was no way to avoid them. They dominated the news cycle and filled cyberspace with repeated updates and commentary. Each of them alone is a tragedy but, collectively, they serve as an awakening that we can't go on with business as usual. I've had hard conversations with my children about all of these events, and in each talk my husband and I tried to emphasize the action part of the dialogue. Something terrible has happened; what are we going to do about it? We sent supplies to one, water to another, and we protested and marched in others. It is our responsibility to create a home environment that encourages our children's curiosity, calms their fears, and extends their thinking around hard and sometimes uncomfortable topics. Creating opportunities to connect your family's life with broader and deeper issues in the world is how you create ripples of change.

Of course we want to create a home that is safe and loving. We want our children to grow up feeling loved and nurtured. We want our children to leave our homes being confident and independent thinkers. To get them to that stage of their lives, we have to pour into them the ingredients that support a healthy and successful launch. You are the first person that they will come to with their big questions, the first person they will reach out to, asking for support and encouragement. Don't let your fears drown out their need to question a world that is sometimes frightening and unfair, and in some cases bigoted and racist. It is our responsibility to invest in our children through continuous open dialogue and active listening. It is our job to walk them through the scariness. It is our obligation to teach our children to stand up and be allies for groups that are marginalized and silenced.

Establishing these practices in your home early and often is key to consistent and trusting dialogue, which will be essential as they become teenagers. (Trust me on this!) So how do you actually go about having a big conversation? Let me share a few key strategies that will help you navigate the dialogue and, hopefully, support a positive experience for you and your children.

Listen and be attentive. When you begin these conversations, make sure you are present and actively listening. This may require less talking! Resist the temptation to work at finding solutions for your children. Instead, listen with the intent to hear and understand their feelings. Don't jump in and try to fix the issue or attempt to have the "right" answers to their questions. It may even be appropriate for you to say, "Do you need me to only listen or would you like my opinion/advice when you are done?" This is especially useful when speaking with teens.

Listen to their questions with genuine interest and care. Children have important and valuable perspectives that should be heard, even if they are different from yours. Learning about their viewpoints will ultimately help you learn more about your child, and who doesn't want that? When you speak, get down to their level and look into their eyes, paraphrase what you hear them say, and thank them for coming to you to ask such important questions. Make sure that what you say after this does not violate the trusting relationship you are trying to build.

Be honest and vulnerable. Open dialogue is about having the courage to have hard conversations with yourself and your children, even when—or especially when—you are fearful. The world is going to continue to go through terrifying times. Your children will ask you about topics you were trying to avoid. Don't be afraid to allow them to ask you hard questions. Remember, you are the role model for what this process looks like. You don't have to have the answers and you won't always know the right thing to say. Conveying this lack of knowledge with authentic emotion teaches a valuable lesson—because your kids aren't always going to know the right thing, either! Being vulnerable and displaying your feelings, and allowing your children to see you deal with various emotions in constructive ways, is an invaluable lifelong gift to them. When you consistently, openly, and honestly show up for your children, they will learn that they, too, can show up as their vulnerable selves.

It's not just what you say; it's how you say it. It's particularly imperative that, without judgment, you acknowledge what your child is feeling. Being critical of what they say or the questions they ask is a sure way to stop them from engaging in open dialogue in the future. As humans, especially as parents, we sometimes speak more loudly with our nonverbal communication, and our children have become well versed at reading what we are feeling without us ever having to open our mouths. Be mindful of your body language and make sure it remains open, inviting, and nonjudgmental. When you speak, be aware of your tone, using a gentle voice and coming from a place of radical love. I always tell my children: Oftentimes it's not what you say that's the issue, it's the way you say it. It's a constant reminder for parents, too. When you speak to your children in a harsh tone or you become aggressive, not only will you not get the desired results, you risk damaging your relationship over time. As the saying goes, respect is earned, and that goes both ways in a parent-child relationship. Children mirror the behavior that they most often see.

Be curious and open to learning. Your lived experiences impact the way you interpret current events and social issues. You won't have the answers to these issues, and you can't be an expert on everything (it's best to bust that myth with your children early). But don't let that stop you from engaging in open dialogue with your family. Set an example for your children as you remain a person who learns, unlearns, and relearns.

My son Ryan used to ask me so many questions I didn't know the answer to that I had him create a book of "WHY." He would bring this spiral binder in the car every day and the minute he asked me questions I couldn't answer on the spot, I told him to write them in his WHY book. When we had a few minutes in the evening we would look up his questions together. He would either write out the answer or print it out and glue it to the page. We both learned so much through the WHY book.

It's okay to admit that you don't know everything. It's also okay to tell your child that you need to think for a little bit and come back to her question later. Take the time you need to educate yourself and reflect, and then make sure you circle back around to have that conversation. This assures your child that their curiosity is important, and it encourages them to continue asking questions and finding answers—and as you listen and learn, you may spark your own curiosity.

Follow up and take action. Most conversations, especially those regarding major events or social justice topics, will happen incrementally over time. Follow-up and action will look different depending on the topic and age of your children. Sometimes follow-up includes clarifying misinformation and gaps your child may have on a topic. It could also include activities you do together, such as reading a book with your child that can help you both process something powerful or painful. Whatever your follow-up looks like, it is vital, as your attention and action will help to keep your child's anxiety and stress to a minimum.

Follow-up offers us and our kids an opportunity for growth. Brainstorm a list of solutions with them. Talk about what could work (or not work) and why. This kind of thought and intention will pay off exponentially as they grow to become change agents in the world. Don't let the fear of not knowing what to say get in the way of having important conversations.

We are pretty deep in this chapter already and I know some of you are questioning how to have these difficult conversations with your children. I see you. There are ways to approach these moments that will make them easier for both you and your children. Here's a quick breakdown of a few key qualities that help facilitate positive conversations:

- **Sensitivity:** Share your feelings in a tender, loving manner.
- **Age-appropriateness:** Break down the hard topics in the simplest terms.
- **Sincerity:** Stay truthful and honest, even when you don't know the answers.
- **Contextualization:** Offer appropriate background information and share examples drawn from their lives that will help them make concrete connections.
- **Curiosity:** Give in to and lead with your children's curiosity instead of your fears and anxieties.

Let's tackle a couple of the hard ones together.

TACKLING THE HARD STUFF

I asked parents from my social media platforms what they thought was the most difficult topic to discuss with their children, and I got a lot of feedback. Topics parents worried about ranged from violence, racism, sexism, money, hate, pornography, and child trafficking to neurodiversity. I've selected a few of the top responses below to use as examples and offer sample scripts for opening up a dialogue.

The advice that follows is based on my professional and educational background (I hold a doctorate and master's degree in education and a bachelor's degree in family and child sciences), as well as my most important education credential: twenty years at motherhood university. I am not a trained clinical psychologist. If you think your children or your family would benefit from speaking to a trained therapist, please make sure you seek out a qualified practitioner. Taking care of your family is the most important goal of Social Justice Parenting.

Death. We've all experienced the pain of death. During the height of the global COVID-19 pandemic, many of us lost loved ones and watched as the death rate in the country (and globally) rose steadily for months on end. Death is unavoidable, and your children, if they haven't already, will one day have to deal with terrible loss. You can make that loss more bearable if you give them an opportunity to view and accept death as a normal part of life. Experts recommend introducing death into ordinary experiences with your children. That way, your children will have some background knowledge before they have to make sense of losing someone close to them, like a grandparent or a pet. A teachable moment could be when you find a dead bug or critter when you're outside together. It would be a great time to talk about the cycle of life and explain that death is a part of it, and that as we get older our bodies just stop working.

When I think back to my own children's experiences around the age of ten, I recall three of my five children coming to me crying as they thought about the reality that I was going to die at some point. This is so painful, but it's also so normal. When your family is experiencing death, the way you react to your child plays a critical role in their journey of grieving and healing. Make sure your responses are simple and direct and convey permanence. Young children often don't fully understand that death isn't reversible. Use straightforward language and keep it as clear as you can. Experts frown on using euphemisms while explaining death to young kids. Phrases like "in a better place," "passed away," "putting her to sleep," or "went home" can confuse young children. These phrases soften the truth, but they can actually backfire, causing more anxiety around common activities—like a child being afraid to go to sleep in case he won't wake up, or panicking when loved ones travel, fearing they won't come back. Be loving but precise with your language.

"I am so sad. I need to tell you that Grandpa died today." [SENSITIVE]

"What does 'died' mean?"

"When someone or something dies, it means they are no longer alive. They are no longer breathing. Their heart is no longer beating. Which means they don't move, or eat, or do anything. Their body stops working." [AGE-APPROPRIATE]

"Will I die? Will you die?"

"Everyone will die eventually, but it probably won't be for a long time." [SINCERE]

"Where do you go when you die?"

"No one knows for sure, but I believe that (insert your beliefs here). But it's hard to really explain it because we can't experience it for ourselves." [CONTEXTUALIZE] The response to this last question becomes more nuanced based on your religious beliefs. Use the opportunity to discuss your beliefs around death.

"I don't want to go to the funeral. What if I get scared?"

"It's okay to be afraid. I feel afraid, too. Let me tell you what happens at funerals and if at any time you need to leave, you just tell me and I promise I will walk out with you and we can go and sit in the lobby, together. Does that sound like a good plan?" [CURIOSITY]

Be patient, open, and honest. Allow your child to see you grieve, and let your child grieve in whatever way works for them. Keep in mind that everyone grieves differently and your child's grieving can manifest in various forms, including behaviorally, socially, or academically. Talk about how you're feeling and what you're doing to try to feel better. Engage in self-talk out loud so your kids, of all ages, can hear you work through the process by normalizing these universal emotions. Let them know that it takes time to heal after losing someone they loved.

Sexual Assault. I first talked with my children about sexual assault before they turned one year old. I know you may be thinking, "There's no way she can be serious. She is straight up telling a lie." I get it. Let me explain.

Raising children who recognize when something doesn't feel right to them in their bodies begins when you teach your children about body parts. Actively teaching body privacy, where children are clear about the parts of their bodies that are private and shouldn't be looked at or touched by others, begins by using the actual names of body parts. If you don't call it by name, it teaches your child that the private parts of their body are something to hide or something they should be ashamed of. In not naming, you unintentionally teach your children that if someone touches them there, it may not be safe to tell you or a trusted adult since even saying the real name of my private part out loud was too scary, even for Mommy. Side note: During those private "show-and-tell" moments in our kindergarten classes, we defined "private parts" as anything that your bathing suit covers. That could be a great way to start the dialogue if you have little ones.

In normalizing body parts, you are creating a shame-free zone for having dialogue that supports body autonomy and agency. You are teaching your children that they are the boss of their body and have the right (and responsibility) to make decisions about it. It also creates a safe space for your children to talk about it and share if something happens to them. They need to be assured that it's not their fault and that they are not responsible when another person violates them in any way. My kids and I were hanging out in the family room one evening, watching TV. There was a commercial that caused me to hit pause on the remote. All heads whipped in my direction. Teenagers began to display symptoms of the eye-rolling disease. They knew Mama-teacher was about to enter the room! I live for the teachable moments.

"Can we have a quick conversation about what was on TV? I need to know that you know I will always have your back. This is really important to me." [SENSITIVE]

"You all know that if anyone ever touches you in ways that make you uncomfortable or hurts you that you can come to me and tell me, right?" [AGE-APPROPRIATE]

In unison, which they did so well at this age, they replied. "Yes, Mom."

"And do you know there may even be a chance that your body will respond like it likes it because that's the way we were created, but it still isn't your fault and you still should tell me, right?" [sideways looks by the kids at each other] [AGE-APPROPRIATE]

"Yes, Mom?"

"And you know even if they tell you I won't believe you, you know I always will, right? Because there is nothing more important to me than the five of you. And you know I will ALWAYS believe you. ALWAYS! Even if you said it was Dad [sideways look from Dad—me, sheepish grin back to the hubby]. Sorry babe, I'm just saying . . . I love you, but even if they said it was you. [back to the kids] You know I will always believe you and always fight to keep you safe from anyone, right?" [SINCERE]

"Yes, Mom."

"You know to get you not to tell, a perpetrator will say things like they will hurt me or you or someone you love if you tell. They will even tell you that it's your fault or that you really liked it to get you not to tell me. It's a way that they manipulate you to keep it a secret, but none of it is true." [CONTEXTUALIZE]

"Yes, Mom."

"Okay, I need to hear from each of you while you are looking in my eyes. Alexandra, do you know I will fight until the ends of the earth to keep you safe and you can trust that I will always have your back?"

"Yes, Mommy. I do."

"Trace, do you . . ."

"Yes, Mom. Yes, Mom." [my cue that I am now taking too long making my point]

"Tyler?"

"Yes, Mom."

"Ryan?"

"Yes, Mom."

"Dylan?"

"Yes, Mom."

"Okay, love you all . . . any questions that you want to ask me?" [CURIOSITY]

"No, Mom. Can we get back to the movie?"

That was that. Until three days later, when my youngest son, seven at the time, came to me at bedtime and said, "Thank you, Mom, for keeping us safe and believing us." OMG! My love for this kid was too much to be contained in my heart at that moment. He heard me, and he felt my absolute, unconditional radical love.

Sometimes it will feel like you're talking to yourself, like your children aren't really listening or processing (or even caring about) what you're saying to them. You won't be the first parent who's felt this. Each one of us in the Movement of Moms has felt like they are talking to an empty room—trust me, you're not. They're listening, so just keep talking.

Another conversation about sexual assault that my family engaged in was talking to my sons about their role in breaking the cycle of "boys will be boys" or "locker room talk," which is not only offensive but could lead to a life-altering assault on the women who will be in their lives. My three youngest sons and I were driving home from school, and they were ages nine, eleven, and twelve at the time. As we entered into my neighborhood there was an update on NPR on the Brett Kavanaugh hearing. I pulled into the driveway (one of many NPR Driveway Moments!) and turned the volume up and asked my sons to listen. After several minutes of quiet listening, I switched the radio off and turned to my boys in the back seat.

"This story makes me both angry and sad. I need you to know why. And I want to hear what feelings you have about it." [SENSITIVE]

The boys, very wide-eyed, looked back at me so intently. They wanted to make sure I knew they were listening to what made me so emotional.

"Do you know what Brett Kavanaugh is being accused of? Do you know what sexual consent means and why it's so important for us to listen to the victim's story?"

Although they couldn't articulate a clear definition, they knew it was related to the #MeToo movement, which we had already talked about in our home. "Sexual assault is when someone touches another person's private body parts without their permission, even when the person says no." [AGE-APPROPRIATE]

That day in the car, we also talked a lot about what "No" means. "It's really important to me that you understand our expectations for you as young men. I need to know that you will always treat girls the way you want Dad to treat me and the way you would want your sister to be treated." [SINCERE] "There may be times when you have to stand up for and support girls when your friends are not being respectful."

We role-played various ways that "No" still means "No," even when the word is not used.

> "What if she says, 'I don't really feel comfortable with your hand there?' What if she says, 'It feels nice, but I am not ready?' What if she says yes, but she was drinking?" [CONTEXTUALIZE]
>
> In perfect chorus, my boys sang, "It still means no!"
>
> What I said to them next surprised them. "What if you tell her no?"
>
> They giggled at first before realizing I was still in my mama-teacher zone. "What if she wants to kiss you and you don't feel comfortable? What if your friends make fun of you because you weren't ready?"
>
> My twelve-year-old replied, "Does that happen?"
>
> "Yes, that's a different perspective that you don't hear a lot of people talking about. We can brainstorm ideas on what you would say if you are ever in this situation." [CURIOSITY]

Conversations about sexual consent don't just have to happen with your daughters. This is a dialogue that your sons have to be a part of in order to change the culture around sexual assault in society.

Poverty and Homelessness. "Mom, why is that man pushing that grocery cart full of old things down the street? He needs to go home and take a shower. He's so dirty. Why is he so dirty, Mom?"

This unexpected question from her five-year-old daughter left her mother, Shelby, frozen. She wasn't prepared to answer it and she certainly wasn't prepared for the stares that she received from the other customers in the Target parking lot. Embarrassed, she shushed her daughter, grabbed her hand, and quickly got in her car.

Have you ever been in a situation like this, where your child says something that makes you feel like your parenting skills are being put on full display? We often allow our egos or our fear of judgment to get in the way of our children's natural inquisitiveness. Children notice just about everything, and their observations and perceptions about the world, including its flaws and imperfections, are more accurate and resilient than our weak attempts to protect them from uncomfortable situations or hard topics. Protecting your children from the realities of poverty may be your first instinct. I get it. You may think it might be too disturbing for them to grapple with, or it may make them sad to know people are hungry, hurting, and homeless. But I'll say it again: Even though it may be uncomfortable for you, always tell them the truth.

In this case, talking about homelessness is a good time to demonstrate empathy and recognition of others' hardships. Answer their questions directly. "Some people don't have enough money to pay for a house." "He doesn't have any place to go to shower or to keep all of his things." When your children are young, it's important to answer their questions directly without complicating the dialogue. Remember, age-appropriate response is part of your dialogue.

Shelby was given an opportunity to help shape her daughter's understanding and to teach her empathy, but she let her social discomfort and her fear of getting it wrong stand in the way. Our upbringing and childhood experiences may shape the way you think about topics like poverty and homelessness. When encountering people who appeared homeless, did your family roll up the car windows, cross to the other side of the street, or tell you not to hang around "those" people? If this is the case, it is a good idea to do some self-reflection. If you haven't read the previous chapter on Reflection, this would be a great time to go back to it. Think about your unconscious biases about people who live in economic poverty. Do your initial reactions match the core values that you've established for your family? If you give yourself time for self-reflection, you'll be more prepared to have honest dialogue with your children.

Poverty and homelessness are topics that make children (and many adults) feel uncomfortable. When talking to your children, begin the conversation with a compassionate heart. Never use the homeless person as an "example" of what could happen if you don't do well in school, don't go to college, or don't work hard. Not only does this perpetuate negative stereotypes or misinformation about people living in poverty, but it teaches your children that this person is "bad" or did something to deserve their situation. The goal is to create a space for your children to explore these difficult topics in ways that move them from a state of curiosity and confusion to empowerment and encouragement through social action. The conversation between Shelby and her five-year-old daughter could have gone like this:

"It's upsetting seeing that, isn't it? He's dirty because he doesn't have anywhere to go. He doesn't have a shower because he doesn't have a home." [SENSITIVE]

"What do you mean he doesn't have a home?"

"A lot of people in the world don't have homes. They might have lost their jobs or their jobs don't pay them enough to buy a place to live." [AGE-APPROPRIATE]

"He's scary."

"He might seem scary but he's just a man. He's trying to take care of himself the best way he can right now." [SINCERE]

"Why doesn't he have a home? Can we buy him one? You can use some of my money."

"You are such a kind girl. I'm not sure why he doesn't have a home, but there are some places he can go to get some food and sleep. Maybe we can go help at one of those places or donate money or items to help others. Would you like that?" [CONTEXTUALIZE]

"Why isn't he there right now? Why is he out here with his grocery cart?"

"The shelter is a place for him to get food and to have a safe space for him to sleep at night. I think he still has to go out during the day, just like we do. Would you like to give him this water bottle and granola bar? Would you like to do that?"

"I don't really want to."

"That's okay, I can give it to him. Maybe next time." [CURIOSITY].

When my oldest children were seven and five, on our way to school we encountered people who would come up to our car with their signs at the same traffic light each day. My children had a lot of questions. "Why are they asking for money? Why don't they have a house?" I think the question that changed everything was the day my son asked, "Do they have children?" This brought both my children and me to tears. My children couldn't fathom that there were children without a safe place to live or food to eat. For months my son would always grab an extra snack on our way to school to give to the person standing on that corner. Every time we went to the grocery store he would want to get extra. He often asked to go to the local deli to buy sandwiches for them.

My children's kindergarten teacher, Mrs. Herman, noticed kids talking about it in class, and she created an entire unit on what kids can do to help their neighbors. She read books and brought in the director of the local food bank to answer questions for the kindergarten class. Mrs. Herman brought in a large container and collected change from the students to raise money for community members in need. The children did extra chores at home, set up lemonade stands on the weekends, and made and sold arts and crafts to family and friends to raise money. After raising hundreds of dollars, the class took a field trip to the local grocery store to purchase the items that the shelter needed. We caravanned to the shelter and the children were able to put the food that they purchased on the shelves in the pantry. This had a profound impact on my children.

Young children's natural inclination is to take action. They want to know what they can do to help, so have a list of ideas that your family can do together, like donating toys, books, pet supplies, or food to nonprofit organizations. (Always ask the organization in advance what is needed so your efforts will have the biggest impact.) Give that list to your child and empower them to do the shopping with you.

As children get older (generally speaking, ten and up, though you know your kid best), they start to show a deeper curiosity about the world around them, and they are more equipped for a richer, more complex understanding of homelessness and poverty. They listen to your words, but more important, they pick up on your nonverbal cues. When you encounter a panhandler on the street, what does your body language say to your children? Do they see empathy or annoyance? Your reaction conveys your values. Do these values align or conflict with the core values that you've established with your family? Don't shy away from discussing your feelings and answering their questions about poverty and homelessness, and don't shy away from starting these conversations.

This can also help you establish conversations around explaining how and why you respond the way you do. Get honest here. Explain why you give or don't give money to the person in need. If you are more comfortable giving food or donating to the local shelter, explain that to your children. Maybe you're not comfortable with interacting with people who are homeless at all. You owe it to your children to explain that as well. Use as many teachable moments as possible—watching the news/TV/internet, encountering panhandlers, driving through different neighborhoods—to guide your discussion. Ask them why they think there are so many people who live in poverty or are homeless. Hearing their initial thoughts will give you an idea of where to start. These are a few major categories that have come up in conversations with my children about why people are homeless and live in economic poverty:

- Lack of affordable housing and fair wages
- Inadequate support for veterans
- Lack of resources for immigrants
- Struggles with mental health and addiction
- Lack of a safe space for victims of abuse and discrimination
- Major life change (divorce, natural disasters, death, coming out, etc.)

And remember, you are not required to have all the answers. Research with your children. Learn together and decide how your family can take action on this extremely vital concern in our communities. Some families purchase Thanksgiving or Christmas meals for other families. Our family gets wish lists from one of the local group homes and purchases presents during the holiday season. Another idea is collecting items for back-to-school backpacks and winter bags (blankets, gloves, socks, etc.) for individuals without shelter. Although these ideas are helpful to get your children involved, as adults we need to think about the systemic issues that exist and that are instrumental in sustaining the economic gap in our country and in the world. We can't solve poverty and homelessness in one conversation, but we can explore perspectives through open dialogue. Children want to be a part of a solution, and that requires active hope, empathy, and activism.

PAYING ATTENTION

You'll have your own list of tough topics, but you'll find that some you never thought of will make their way into your life. When my friend Sarah's four-year-old was accidentally terrified by the creepy internet meme Momo, it prompted a conversation about online safety a lot earlier than she had planned. Knowing what kinds of conversations are needed with your children requires you to pay attention. I'm not suggesting you eavesdrop on your children . . . nope, I'm not saying that. But I am telling you that you need to be alert and vigilant about your children's lives—their friends, their conversations, their activities. When you're driving your child and his friends around and they're chattering away in the back seat, tune in every now and then. When your daughter is talking to her friend on the phone while lying on the couch and you're in the kitchen cooking dinner, pay attention. If your child casually mentions in passing something that happened at school or something that's going around on the internet, keep that information in your back pocket.

Timing is everything. Hold on to this information until you need it. (Unless you're like me and you blurt it out and call an emergency family meeting. I don't advise this.) Try to control your impulses and wait until a natural moment to bring up the topic, without freaking anybody out.

BUILD YOUR VILLAGE

Finally, I think it's important to create a trusting village to fly with you. Surround yourself with other people who can serve as confidants for your children. There may be times when those other people in your village feel more like a safe space to your child than you or your partner. That may not feel very good for you, but do your best not to take it personally—it doesn't mean that you're doing something wrong. You're not! You are creating a wall of protection around your child that allows them to grow and be independent of you, all while remaining in a safe, loving environment with people who want the best for them.

My village includes my family of sisters, nieces, and brothers-in-law. It also includes friends who have become family. The mother of my godchildren was once my undergraduate student. After she finished my class, I hired her to be my babysitter for my little ones. She became a little sister to me, while becoming a big sister to my daughter. I know if my daughter ever needs to talk to someone, Sember will always be there for her, and because she knows my family's core values (which are very similar to her own), the advice that she gives will be in alignment with the way I value the world.

Build your village. We are so much better together.

GETTING STARTED

Here are open-ended questions/statements to support you in having conversations around any of these topics with your children. Just make sure you are choosing the questions that support you having positive, open dialogue.

- Thank you for sharing. Tell me more.
- That makes me feel ____. How do you feel? Tell me why.
- What would you do?
- How do you think you would feel if that happened to you?
- How would you ask for help?
- Where did you learn that?
- What's another perspective on that topic? What do you think they are thinking?
- How can we explore this more? How can we learn more about this?
- What do you think? Why do you think that?
- I'm so glad we are talking about this. Can we talk more?
- Why do you think people think that way?
- What can our family do to change things?
- What's our responsibility to help with this?
- What would you say to him/her/them if you had a chance?

ENCOURAGING CONTINUOUS OPEN DIALOGUE

I love a teachable moment. I will use any moment to engage in open dialogue with my kids, and as they get older, I notice that they are beginning to do the same. If the children see something on their phones that interests them, they'll come find me in the house to talk about what they are seeing and how they feel about it. Sometimes it's a snippet from pop culture, or a meme, or a clip from their favorite YouTuber or gamer, but often it's politics or social justice issues.

These teachable moments are anchored with regular check-ins. Find a time that works for your family. It could be right before bedtime (we've tried that one, but I noticed that we often go past bedtime—I think my kids may have a career in professional bedtime manipulating). Car rides are great places for these conversations because you have a captive audience, and if the radio is on, conversations about the news may arise naturally. We also use our Sunday dinner time to have deeper conversations.

When we start talking over each other, I bring out our talking stick—a tool used in many Indigenous cultures to support respect and turn taking in conversation. If you aren't holding the stick, your ears are open and your lips are closed. When you establish the safe space rules, make sure everyone understands and knows the consequences for breaking them. One of the most important rules for our family is emphasizing the sacredness of each person's voice and perspective. My older children will sometimes dismiss or make light of their younger siblings' contributions to the conversation. And sure, sometimes their answers are silly or surface level, but other times we get an amazing understanding of their perspective. My rule is that as long as they answer the prompt (even if the answer is not what you wanted or expected), the safe space rules apply.

When my family first started this practice, I found myself correcting their answers or behaviors or telling them to "say more" or "give a real answer." It's important to resist the impulse to overparent or overdirect during this time. Trust me, there will be times when you see or hear things that make you want to pull your hair out or poke your eyes with a toothpick. Seriously, with no exaggeration. There will be times when you just want to NEVER do it again. But don't quit. Don't let those arm-crossing tweens or those eye-rolling teens stop you! Allow them to come around to seeing that this is truly a safe space to air their thoughts and feelings. They will get the hang of it, and over time the conversations will get less silly (like someone responding with "I like the smell of my farts" as they test the "safe place to say anything" rule). And to be honest, we've made some great memories in those moments of silliness. I recommend only discussing one topic or pulling one card from the fishbowl per meeting. Even if they want to do another one, don't do it. It builds the anticipation for the next time if you stop before they are ready or before they think they've had enough. If you let them decide that they've had enough, that's what their brains will remember the next time you pull out the jar. Here are nineteen conversation starters to begin establishing a circle of trust for open dialogue with your family.

- What do you think you should learn more of in school today?
- If you could have a conversation with anyone in history, who would it be and why?
- Who do you think you could be nicer to and what would you do?
- If you could only do one thing the rest of your life, what would it be and why?
- If you could turn one room in the house into any kind of room that you wanted, what would it be and describe what it would look like.
- If your favorite object could talk, what would it be and what would it say?
- What are the top three qualities you like in a friend?
- What part of your life makes you the most excited?
- Describe yourself in five words.
- If you were a superhero, what would be your name and what would be your superpower?
- If you could be famous, what would you want to be famous for?
- What's one rule that you wish we didn't have in the house?
- What's your greatest fear?
- If you could make someone nice, who would it be?
- If you opened a store, what would it be called and what would you sell?

- What's one thing that you want to change about the world?
- If you can ask anyone in the family a question, who and what would you ask?
- What five things would you take with you on a deserted island?
- What's the hardest thing about being you?

CHAPTER 6

COMPASSION

> Our human compassion binds us to one another—not in
> pity or patronizingly, but as human beings who have
> learnt how to turn our common suffering into hope for
> the future.
>
> —Nelson Mandela

I was having a really stressful day. Hard deadlines at work, multiple meetings, driving kids to all the things, then came home from the kids' evening practices to flooding in the bathroom, laundry room, and two of their bedrooms. The water heater had been leaking for the last four hours. My husband was working late and I was left alone to deal with the mess. After finally getting everything cleaned up, kids fed, and homework completed, I was mentally exhausted. I lay down on the couch and I cried. Not an out-of-control, screaming cry, just an exhale, tears rolling down my face kind of cry, totally exhausted from my marathon day. Dylan, my youngest, came over to me, gently wiped my tears, and curled up on the couch to snuggle with me. He held my hand and didn't say a word, just stayed with me, in silence. It was such an emotionally bonding moment for us. I can't say if this compassion and care is the result of nature or nurture (or both), but

I can tell you, I felt cared for and loved at that moment by my then seven-year-old.

RAISING COMPASSIONATE KIDS

There are many definitions of the word "compassion," and it is often intertwined with both empathy and kindness. Researchers at UC Berkeley define compassion as "the feeling that arises when you are confronted with another's suffering and you feel motivated to relieve that suffering." For me, it is that space between our natural ability to be emotionally moved to see things from someone else's perspective (empathy) and taking action to help relieve someone's distress or to lift someone's spirits (kindness/altruism). Research has shown that when we feel compassion—which is a part of human nature, rooted in biology—we release more oxytocin (also known as the "love hormone"), promoting bonding and commitment, our heart rate slows down, and the brain's reward center lights up. It turns out that being compassionate causes a cascade of chemical responses in our body that encourage us to be more compassionate.

Compassion is a feeling. Just like anger, joy, and sadness, compassion serves a purpose—it drives most of us to take action. This doesn't mean that compassion always feels good. Witnessing the suffering of others is painful. For example, every time I see the video of Elijah McClain, a young, unarmed black man who died after being placed in a choke hold by police officers while he was walking home from the store to get iced tea, my heart feels deep pain. Compassion provokes a positive action, but it doesn't *feel good* in the way that happiness or pride does. For me, that makes it all the more important. I wonder sometimes if so many people in this world turn away from compassion because it hurts. I have made it a priority to encourage my children to sit with their compassion and really feel it. I don't want them to turn away from it, no matter how uncomfortable or heavy it gets.

I pay close attention to this with my sons (and my husband). As males, the world tells them to swallow their emotions or to "man up" when they feel them starting to rise. I want them to embrace those big feelings and use them to comfort others. Also, in my interactions while coaching parents or students in my parenting courses, I encourage parents to get comfortable with being uncomfortable. For example, when you want to be an ally, you have to take on the pain of those being discriminated against. You can't turn away when it gets uncomfortable or if you don't like what you see or feel. Let's get real here: Members of the Black community don't get that option. Compassion for others makes us linger, lean in, and absorb someone else's life circumstances.

A local principal makes space for students at her school to linger in these feelings of empathy and compassion. She has created a "Peace Table" in her office. This is a safe space to unpack feelings, resolve conflict, and process the emotions that are sometimes overwhelming. Children can sit at the Peace Table to find peace within (through meditation and/or prayers) or they are allowed to ask to sit at the Peace Table to talk about their feelings with the principal. The Peace Table was created especially for students who have conflict with each other. The students sit at the table together and begin by completing the Peace Table prompts. The prompts could include sentence starters like:

- I felt_____when_____.
- What should have happened was_____.
- You may have felt_____when I_____.
- Next time I will _____ before I _____.
- You should have asked me to_____before you_____.

Once the students have completed the appropriate sentence starter, they began to have dialogue around not just what they were feeling but also what the other person was feeling. What I find interesting about the Peace Table is that this principal never forces the students to apologize or agree. Instead, she allows them to process their emotions and resolve the conflict through honest dialogue. She teaches them that sometimes you walk away from situations agreeing to disagree and that's okay. It's a fantastic lesson in setting healthy boundaries that we all can use in our lives and in witnessing other people's experiences, which helps foster empathy and compassion.

COMPASSION STARTS WITH ME

As with everything else in this book, it has to start with you. Self-compassion is giving ourselves grace when we fail, suffer, or feel like we aren't enough. It's about accepting our flaws and imperfections as a part of our humanity, not a glitch in our personal DNA. Unfortunately, self-compassion is one of the most challenging forms of compassion. Many of us are hardest on ourselves, which can make us feel ashamed and isolated. In a world that needs so much from each of us, we often experience guilt about responding to our own needs and struggles.

In a moment of vulnerability, I need to say this is a place where I struggle. A lot. As a coach in the parenting space, it's difficult not to pick apart my own parenting practices. I question decisions that I make as a mom, especially if they end up not being the best ones for my kids. Every time my children don't listen, don't respond the way I think they should, make mistakes, feel sad. Every time I scream at my children, forget to sign a paper, or forget to show up at an event. Every time I react to my husband in a way that is not patient or thoughtful and my children see it. Every time I am not consistent with chores or taking away electronics when I need thirty more minutes of time to finish something at work. Yes, I do all of those things, too. I self-critique instead of engaging in self-compassion. So when I write this book, I am coming from a place of "work in progress." You are not alone in your fears and doubts and struggles. My best friend has to remind me, "Traci, you always talk about grace. Are you giving yourself grace?" And you know what comes next for me . . . I circle back on the ideas of radical love.

As an activist, it's also easy for me to critique my commitment to the social justice issues that are important to me. With all of the racial injustice that our country is experiencing (and has experienced since our country's inception, really—our awareness is just catching up), I question if I'm doing enough. Is my way of teaching about anti-racism effective? Am I reaching enough people, am I finding a way to do the work and still stay focused on my family? I sometimes feel like my message isn't "radical" or "loud" enough, or it doesn't push people enough. When the work gets to be too much for my empath disposition, I need to take a break. But then I feel guilty about taking the time to recharge and recenter myself: Injustice doesn't take a break. What makes me think I deserve one? The mean girl inside says, "How can you spend your time being worried about yourself when you're neglecting so many people who need help?" I do my best to ignore that voice, but it's not always easy. It helps that I have a partner who is able to talk me through these big emotions, reminding me to breathe.

I know I'm not alone in this. It's a universal problem, especially for moms. Sacrificing, being superwoman, caring for our children at our own expense, and giving our time and talent to our community—these are all socialized traits of being a "good" mother, but they leave very little time for self-compassion. The funny thing is, the more compassionate you are to yourself, the more helpful you can be to others. We all must learn to tell that inner mean girl to take a back seat and, instead, treat yourself like a best friend. Be tender, gentle, forgiving, and kindhearted.

I try to stay in a continuous cycle of reflection. I constantly work at putting less of my energy into worrying about what I can't control or what's in the past. When you're continuously focused on the things you're unhappy with, you become unable to show yourself compassion. You are less able to grow and transform. Self-compassion allows you to move past mistakes and to embrace all the good inside you.

Many of the moms that I work with are trying to do the work of unpacking and understanding their childhood experiences with racism. My client Lisa, in particular, was dealing with a lot of anxiety around her childhood, anxiety that she realized kept her in a cycle of fear-based parenting. She had been raised in a home that was steeped in racist ideology. She told me about how terribly her mother treated their housekeeper, and how she looked down on all the Black people in her community. She cried to me about the beliefs she had internalized, like believing that the role of Black people in society was to serve people like her and her family.

Although Lisa had long ago left those ways of thinking behind, she would often get stuck playing them over and over, having this narrative on repeat in her mind. We discussed ways that she could move forward, how to have those conversations with her children, and came up with a plan to involve her family in anti-racist activities in their community. This was a way to channel that negative experience into something positive. When those self-recriminating feelings come up, as they will continue to do, she is able to give herself grace and to focus on the new narrative that reveals all the positive and thoughtful ways that she's been combating racism. She has been consciously raising her children to have constructive experiences

around race-related issues and intentionally exposing them to opportunities to do better in the world.

When you model this kind of self-compassion, you are doing an
enormous service for your children. None of us is perfect, and all of
us have room in our lives for improvement. But in order to do better,
we have to accept ourselves where we are. You deserve compassion,
rooted in radical love. That is an incredible message to pass on to your
children.

COMPASSION IN THE HOME

Compassionate homes are places where children's voices and feelings
are prioritized. Everything starts with the family. By the age of three,
children begin to show genuine compassion and empathy and are
able to understand that their feelings and experiences can be different
from those of others. The ability to care for and about other people
is within us all, but young children need support in connecting these
innate feelings to the people around them. Compassion is something
that is nurtured and modeled through your love and care.

Compassion is not something we tell our children; instead, it
shows up in our everyday behaviors and actions. Your kids watch
closely to see how you respond to situations, even when you think
they aren't paying attention. You want them to witness the way you
see the good in everyone, no matter how small the issue or who the
person is. For example, I want my children to want to help and support each other more often without having to be "told" to do it. I
sometimes say, "How do you think your brother would feel if he came
back in the room and saw that we had cleaned up the room for him?"
Even the youngest child can get used to the idea of putting herself in
another's shoes. Creating opportunities that build capacity for compassion can be incorporated into your daily routine.

Mom: I'm fixing sandwiches. What kind do you want?

Son: Turkey, please.

Mom: What should I make for your brother?

Son: Turkey.

Mom: Let's think about that. That is definitely the sandwich that you want because it's your favorite. Let's think about your brother. How would you think he would feel if he came home and saw *your* favorite sandwich made for him? What would you think he would say about the sandwich that he wanted?

Son: Peanut butter and jelly!

Mom: Yes, I love how you thought about your brother's feelings and what would make him feel happy.

Small, daily gestures can really impact the way your children show up for others. I often hear parents say that their greatest wish for their children is for them to be happy and successful. I believe raising children who are compassionate offers greater value to the world—and to themselves.

One time my family was in the drive-through line of a restaurant and the person behind us was blowing her horn and screaming out her window that we were taking too long. And yeah, in her defense, with five children we do take a long time, even though it's always the same menu! But she was being obnoxious. When I got to the window, I paid our bill and then paid for the impatient woman's bill as well. My children were shocked. They couldn't believe I was paying for her food. They asked, "Why did you pay for her? She was so rude!" I explained that we didn't know her circumstances and that maybe she needed some love, compassion, and kindness that day and we were in a position to give her that. After we left the drive-through we were stopped at a traffic light when the woman pulled up next to us, rolled down her window, and very kindly said, "Thank you and God bless. I was coming to get some lunch for my son who just got off of work. I only had three dollars but he needed some help." I just smiled and nodded my head. Again, nothing earth-shattering, but the message was clear. In that moment, I chose to see a good person having a bad day—which turned out to be the truth. We won't always get confirmation of our assumptions, but we should always assume the best. I give this same feedback to moms attending my workshops as we discuss the terms of engagement: Assume good intent. Choosing to see the good in people is compassion in action, and we should never let an opportunity go by where compassion can be given or received. In order for our children to learn how to put themselves in others' shoes, they have to experience different perspectives and viewpoints over and over again. Once it's habit, they never forget.

My friend Louise from Northern Ireland told me a story about her dad. He made a conscious choice to send his Protestant family to a predominantly Catholic swimming club, at a time when the country was strictly religiously segregated. He wanted his family to have a wider lens of the world, to be able to see perspectives and to expand the love in their hearts to include others. These values impacted the way Louise viewed the world, and compassion has become a core value for her in raising her own children.

I always see my son Ryan watching me when one of his siblings or someone in the community (often at the grocery store or driving) does something that has the potential to trigger me. I can feel his eyes peering through me. Now I would like to say I always respond appropriately and model the proper ways to deal with frustration or disappointment. But you know the reality is that, like everyone,

I sometimes don't show up as my best self. But I try to be consistent with modeling compassion, even when *I* didn't make the best choice. If you recall, the process of "owning your own junk" is one of our family rules. It means I have to take time to think about how I felt and reacted in the moment (self-compassion) and then take ownership of my responsibility and see the situation from multiple perspectives (compassion for others). This is how we teach our children compassion and empathy. When I have not modeled my best behavior, I go to my child and say, "I want to apologize for the way I responded. I should have walked away or taken a few deep breaths first to give myself time to think. If I could do it again I would have said how angry I was, but not in the way that I did." I own my own junk! I apologize to them, but I don't beat myself up or get overly dramatic about it. I recognize that I sometimes screw up (this goes back to recognizing the humanity in myself) and give myself grace. This is such important modeling, too, because it helps them understand that they, too, can sometimes have bad moments and that it will be okay.

You can prove that to them by showing compassion when your children make mistakes. Remember, our kids generally don't purposefully hurt or annoy their siblings, maliciously defy their parents, or intentionally create issues for themselves or those around them. All of these things happen from time to time, but it's not helpful or compassionate to assign malicious intent. I let my children know that the action in question was not acceptable, but I love them and want to support them in moving forward with a plan.

I've seen how they have taken my example and used it in their interactions with each other. One day Ryan was trying to be helpful by cutting the grass. He took the oil can instead of the gasoline can from the garage and filled the lawn mower's gas tank with oil. When my husband came outside and saw what happened, let's just say he wasn't happy! Dylan quickly stepped in and said, "It's okay, Ryan. Dad, he didn't mean to do it. Everybody makes mistakes." I loved the way Dylan went right into "you are your brother's keeper" mode. When I talked to Dylan later, he said his heart felt sad for Ryan and he knew how upset he would feel if he had made that mistake.

Each day is a clean slate. Your children need to feel your forgiveness each time they make mistakes, each time they've had a bad day. They need to feel like they are never defined by a negative thing that they've done. There is great power in forgiveness, and it goes both ways. Telling our children when we were wrong and asking them to forgive us is not giving up power—it is actually empowering your children to be more compassionate and empathic human beings. And when we forgive them, we are granting them power that they need to do better next time. After the lawn mower incident, my husband had to ask for forgiveness. He had to step back and think about our son's motive or intent, then forgive himself for the way he responded (self-compassion), and finally to go back to Ryan and apologize for the way he reacted (compassion).

It can also be helpful to create authentic compassionate teaching moments. When watching a movie or reading a book together, ask your child about what the main character was feeling. "They didn't invite Emily to the party. I wonder how that made her feel? How do you think you would feel if that happened to you?" In these moments, you're building their capacity for compassion. I even try to create compassion in doing chores (and bonus . . . you get a clean house). When my kids were younger, I would have them help each other with cleaning up their rooms. It would have been just as easy to have each child clean their own rooms, but helping each other begins to build a bond of community, connection, and compassion in the house. It shows them how much they need each other and how great it feels to help others and be helped. We would set the timer for ten minutes and then we would all clean one room together. Then we would re-set the timer for another ten minutes and clean the next room. It's amazing how much you can get done in ten minutes with six pairs of hands working together! Sometimes we even laughed and enjoyed the time together (not always, but it was nice when it happened).

I ask my children to think about chores this way: If they don't do them, who will have to? Obviously, the answer is Mom! If they still aren't getting it, I'll spark their compassion for me by saying, "I feel sad that I have to clean the entire house. I won't get a chance to play with you all. I won't get a chance to relax and read my book. If *you* don't pick up your dirty clothes from the bathroom floor, *someone* will have to do it and it would be so nice if you made sure it wasn't always the same someone." This often resonated with them and they began to be more proactive about doing their share. "If I do this, then Mom would be able to do that. She deserves to do that." That's how I was able to get this book written! My kids felt compassion for me while I sat in my chair for hours at a time with my face staring at the computer. They supported each other and got their chores done. This was the greatest act of compassion a mother could ask for!

Raising children who are grounded, and not entitled, is impor-tant to me. Studies show that children who grow up with a sense of entitlement—which comes from overparenting, overindulging, and over-purchasing for your children—are more concerned about them-selves, show less compassion and empathy for others, lack a strong work ethic, and may behave as if rules don't apply to them. Showing and teaching compassion to your children requires you to start say-ing NO sometimes. NO, you're not going to clean up after them. NO, you're not going to buy them that thing they want. NO, you're not going to be spoken to in that way. Giving consequences to their actions will support their ability to see situations from various view-points. If your child calls his sibling a name, do not let it slide. "I feel [insert your feelings] when you talk to your brother that way. Being kind to your brother is a rule in our house. Calling him [insert name] is unacceptable and there are consequences for that behavior."

The go-to consequence in our house is the cell phone. Mama's line is, "If you can't show compassion or communicate with love to the people in this house, then you don't get the chance to do it with your friends." I've also been known to say something like, "Until you can talk to the people in this house with compassion and kindness, you can't talk on the phone." (I can always make that cell phone or gaming box relevant to the crime!) Be consistent with your consequences and show your children that treating people with compassion is important. When they fail to do so, it comes at a price. Learning this in the home is a great start for the necessary work of acts of kindness in the world (more on this in the next chapter!). Here are some things to think about:

- **Enforce boundaries:** Saying no to your children teaches them that they won't always get what they want. This is just a part of life, and it will help them learn how to recover from disappointments, which in turn builds the capacity to have compassion for others who have setbacks. During the breakdowns, acknowledge the feelings instead of rewarding the temper tantrum or negative behavior. "I see you are disappointed that you couldn't get that toy today." "I know you are angry that you aren't allowed to go to the party, but our rule is there must be a parent present." This demonstrates that you have empathy for them in this situation but you're holding your ground.
- **Make them work:** Working for their allowance or working because they are part of the family (we do the latter in our house) teaches your children to support others, which helps them understand the importance of community and working as a team.

- **Don't worry about being liked:** There are going to be times when your child is angry and disappointed with you. It's okay! Parenting is not about being popular, and they'll get over it. Don't let their behavior determine your rules. Staying firm teaches your children that they have to abide by the same rules as everyone else. This is a foundation for teaching fairness and equity.
- **Encourage gratitude:** Children learn to be grateful when they don't get everything that they ask for. Allow them to want those extra things. Teach them to say thank you (even when it's Aunt Ethel's fruitcake). Have them write grateful journals each day. We have a whiteboard on the front door and the children have to write an answer to a daily question before they leave each day. That question is often centered around gratitude, giving thanks, or being thankful.

COMPASSION WHEN IT'S HARD

There is definitely a movement in schools to incorporate social and emotional curriculum in the classroom, particularly in terms of bullying. While we once thought of bullying as a straightforward dichotomy of good and bad ("bullies are Bad People"), we're now gaining a richer understanding of why bullying happens and what it means. Schools that are run by administrators who operate with compassion can see bullying as the cry for help that it is and respond accordingly. It's so important to seek out the underlying issue of the bullying behavior.

Of course, it's a little more difficult to do when you're the one being bullied—or worse, when you're watching your child being bullied. We get our Mama Bear on and compassion goes out the window. I remember a friend of mine, Annie, telling me a story about her daughter getting bullied in day care. Four-year-old Kyra would come home upset every day, talking about a girl named Chloe who wouldn't share or take turns and would pull Kyra's hair. Kyra's distress triggered Lisa's maternal guilt over putting her child in day care while she worked and eventually Lisa came to feel actual hostility for a little girl she'd never met. How dare she be mean to her sweet Kyra?

Lisa went to talk to the caregiver at the day care and explained her concerns. The caregiver looked at her blankly and said, "This is Chloe?" She pointed to a toddler. Chloe was two. Of course she pulled hair. Of course she didn't share or take turns. Lisa mumbled something, embarrassed, and fled.

When it comes to protecting our kids, we lose our common sense right along with our compassion, and then when reality hits us, we feel a little silly (or embarrassed or guilty). There is *always* a reason for ill behavior, whether it's an age gap, like in Annie's case, or something going on at home or something in between. Hurt people hurt people, and if someone is causing harm, you have to ask yourself: What's going on with them? What's making them react in this way? What is harming *them*? Entering these situations with compassion can change the complexity of the situation, can humanize the bully, and ultimately can protect the bullied.

And what about when your child is the bully? The truth is that none of us is nice all the time, and even when we raise our children to be compassionate and kind, they will sometimes be hurtful, a lot of the time without realizing it. My friend Elizabeth went to her high school reunion not too long ago (I won't rat on her and tell you which reunion it was!). She was approached by a classmate named Heather, whom she barely remembered. Heather seemed nervous to talk to her, and Elizabeth had no idea why. And it came out that Heather had been carrying a memory of an event that Elizabeth didn't remember *at all*. There had apparently been a contest in school and Heather had worked and worked at it and it had meant a lot to her, and Elizabeth had won it handily and had crowed about it, rubbing her victory in Heather's face.

Now, *had* Elizabeth actually rubbed it in her face? Or was she just a teenager who was excited and proud of herself? Maybe, but she hadn't been paying attention to Heather, and it had really hurt Heather's feelings, so much so that she was still bothered by it all these years later. Small things can hurt, and we can cause pain to others without realizing it.

There wasn't really much Elizabeth could say all these years later. She apologized and bought Heather a drink and eventually they laughed it off. But it stuck with her, and she thought back to what she could have done differently at the time. How could she have had more compassion? Could she have simply been more attentive? If she'd been paying attention, she would have realized how much this meant to Heather and would have been more of a graceful winner. So much of compassion is simply paying attention. We get lost in our own experiences, but we can mitigate the harm we unintentionally cause by staying aware of others and paying attention to how our actions might impact them.

It's important to remember that compassion doesn't equal *permission*—you can have compassion for the person and still think that the behavior is not okay and needs to stop. You have to set boundaries that are helpful and safe. Let me tell you a personal story about this. I'm hopeful that my truth can land softly here and that we've built, in Brené Brown's language, a "safe container" for trust. I want to share this story because it may be an example that could help you.

We often have pretty intense conversations in our house around social issues, politics, race issues, and environmental issues. We believe in raising our children to be change agents, to stand up for what's right and to treat everyone with love and dignity. One day my husband, two oldest children, and I were having lively conversations about the issues that were front and center in the 2020 primary election. Most of the time we are all on the same team and align with our core values and beliefs—but we were not all on the same page during the primary. My husband is very rational and well versed in law, history, and politics and is white (wait just a second . . . I promise I'm going somewhere with this). I, on the other hand, am very emotionally driven, empathic, and focused on education, people, and civil rights. I am Black (I know you already know, just making sure you are paying attention here).

My husband and I were talking about race, and the context of the issue was in both our wheelhouses, but we had very different perspectives on it. He was being a rational lawyer and I was being an empathic educator. My oldest kids joined in, and my daughter is as fiery and emotional as I am, and my oldest son is as rational as my husband. We were all having a wonderfully heated discussion, heated enough that we drew the youngest three out of their rooms to figure out what the heck was going on (as a reminder, there are seven of us in the house, so we are naturally pretty loud).

When the younger ones came out to get a front-row seat for the action, we began to calm down a bit, aware of their presence (not because we didn't want them to hear what we were saying, but it just made us realize how much we were talking over each other—hence the increase in volume). As usual, I wanted to make this a teachable moment for the three young boys, so I slowed things down and tried to make the discussion more of a dialogue. The first thing I said was, "Okay, let's take a step back and let me listen again to what you are saying." I refrained from talking over my husband and son (and tried, less successfully, to get my daughter to do the same). I then repeated their key points to assure them that I was listening, though since I strongly disagreed with these points, I'm sure my tone was more than a little skeptical. I said, "I think your point of view is interesting. I don't see it that way. Here's why."

Honestly, what I wanted to do was tell my husband that he was wrong and that his ideology was stupid, but what kind of teachable moment would that have been? I tried to stay calm, show respect, and not get too personal (at least at first). So I said, "We obviously see this very differently and I'm not sure we will agree and that's okay." I went Michelle Obama high, still in my teacher-mom mode. But then my husband said, "You have to be careful not to brainwash the kids, making them only see the world through a Black lens."

Oh NO. I whipped my head around. "Wait . . . what did he just say . . . he did NOT just say that!" Breathe . . . Breathe. Breathe.

In my husband's defense, I was in full-on activist mode and I was going in pretty hard with my "Blackness." But you know, I've been Black my entire life. I let him know that under no circumstance was he able to call me on anything when I was pulling my race card out of my wallet and slapping it on the kitchen counter. I've lived in my Black skin for over fifty years and he has been standing next to Blackness for twenty-five of them. Only I had the right to make the final call when it comes to Blackness in our family!

My husband and I have talked about that conversation since and have looked back at how it unfolded. He was asking me to be mindful of giving my children all perspectives, which is something he values.

But on the night of our argument, I had just one perspective in mind—my own lived experience as a Black woman. I apologized for that, but I stood by my conviction: that lived experience takes precedence when I am raising Black children.

"The children are both Black and white," my husband said.

"Which means they're neither just Black nor just white," I said, "but the reality is that most people will see them as Black."

My husband agreed and apologized. He acknowledged that his white privilege allowed him to believe his kids could behave as freely as he does. He recognized that my lived experience takes priority in our parenting decisions.

This was an exercise in using our passions, experiences, and voices to stand for what we believe in. It was also a great lesson for all of our children. Sometimes compassion for others means standing firm and being okay with standing alone or, at the very least, not agreeing with the status quo. Remember the Peace Table concept? We don't have to agree, but we can be compassionate and exist peacefully.

COMPASSION IN THE COMMUNITY

In our current political and social climate, it is crucial to remain compassionate. If we don't acknowledge the pain and hurt that continues to plague our country, we will continue to cycle through it. In her speech at the 2020 Virtual Democratic Convention, former First Lady Michelle Obama said:

> The ability to walk in someone else's shoes; the recognition that someone else's experience has value, too. Most of us practice this without a second thought. If we see someone suffering or struggling, we don't stand in judgment. We reach out because, "There, but for the grace of God, go I." It is not a hard concept to grasp. It's what we teach our children.

This part of her speech stayed with me long after the convention was over. It made me think about the work that I do and how shining a light on the power of compassion is integral to it. If we look at the landscape of the country, we will find statistics and events that are downright frightening. Hate crime rates in the nation's ten largest cities have been increasing over the last decade. Peaceful protesters are pepper sprayed and beaten. I think, for me, it really called to mind the images and names of all the Black lives that were lost around the time the convention was going on. We saw so much suffering in 2020. George Floyd and his eight minutes and forty-six seconds of struggling to breathe. Ahmaud Arbery fighting for his life when he was just out for a jog. Are you willing to walk in those shoes? Are you willing to allow your children to? It's a life-altering moment when you talk to your children about what happens when there is a lack of compassion for people because of their skin color. It can feel like you're taking away their innocence . . . but it's also reality, and it will ensure that they work to *change* that reality.

When we teach our children to respond to others in a compassionate way, the positive rippling effect of their responses will be evident. We can't always experience what someone else has gone through, but we can look within to connect on a human level. We all have the desire to connect and the capacity to feel for others.

Compassion in a community means coming together around this common idea of seeing others, and trying to understand their lived experiences, in ways that open your heart to showing up for them. In compassionate communities, the needs of all citizens are acknowledged and made a priority. Karen Armstrong, religious scholar and founder of the Charter for Compassion, a network that connects global leaders and organizers to resources, tools, and storytelling to support the creation of more compassionate communities and institutions, suggests that compassion urges us to work untiringly to alleviate the suffering of our neighbors, to wrangle our egos, and to honor the sacredness of every human being, treating everybody, without exception, with absolute justice, equity, and respect. This is how I choose to live my life and how I want to raise my children to live theirs.

By the time children are eight years old, they are able to understand that a person's feelings may not be based on what's going on with them at the moment but instead may be a by-product of their general life circumstances. During this developmental period, children also grow a more concrete understanding and empathy for a group of oppressed people. This is another reason why it's so important to talk to our children about what they are seeing on the news or reading on social media. You can use these moments to model how to show genuine care for others and how to support or speak up for others. Compassion is the root of all social justice work. I feel pretty confident that our children will immediately show their capacity for compassion when given the opportunity—just make sure you are prepared to show yours, too. The more seeds of compassion you sow, the more your children will harvest a life of service for others.

CHAPTER 7

KINDNESS

Do your little bit of good where you are; it's those little
bits of good put together that overwhelm the world.

–Desmond Tutu

After school one day, my three youngest kids and I met a few friends
at a local park. The boys were away from us playing in the trees when
Tyler came running over to tell me that he'd found a twenty-dollar
bill. He was so excited, he screamed, "This is my lucky day!" After
asking around and not finding the owner, he was happy to keep it.
We left the park to run a couple of errands before heading home
for the evening. As we pulled into the shopping plaza's parking lot,
an immigrant family (a dad with two children who were about the
same ages as my three younger ones at the time) was holding a sign
that read, CAN YOU PLEASE HELP US WITH OUR RENT? Without even
thinking about it, Tyler asked me if he could give his twenty dollars to the family. I was a bit shocked because just an hour before he'd
been so excited about finding it, but almost immediately, that shock
transformed into absolute amazement and pride. As we were leaving
the shopping center, I pulled up next to the family. Tyler rolled his
car window down and gave his money to the little boy. When the dad
saw how much money Tyler was handing to his son, his eyes filled

with tears. He lowered his head and said, "Gracias." I believe that was one of Tyler's proudest moments.

WHAT IS KINDNESS?

Kindness is compassion in action, and it can be a powerful tool in overcoming society's greatest challenges. In the midst of the many challenging issues that plague our country and the world—poverty, homelessness, climate change, immigration, gender inequality, civil rights, and racial discrimination—we need kindness now more than ever.

And here's the wonderful thing about kindness: Each act produces waves that extend beyond our consciousness. Whether you spread kindness, receive kindness, or simply witness it, the end result is the same. It becomes a facilitator for more kindness. Tyler's kindness likely changed that family's day in more ways than one. And who knows what kindness it may have sparked in that father or his children, and how it rippled on from there? We can't always know the impact of our acts of kindness, but we must trust that they will create a ripple and let that knowledge be its own reward.

What do acts of kindness look like for kids? It can be as simple as inviting a new classmate to sit at their lunch table or giving a sibling a much-needed hug. It may extend to community-based activities, such as volunteering at a local food bank or donating clothes or toys to a homeless shelter. It also includes looking for opportunities to stand up for others and champion causes. One of my daughter's friends, Rae, uses her social media account to address topics like the Black Lives Matter movement, LGBTQ+, breast cancer, and body positivity. She asks her peers to see the world from a different perspective, and she supports other teens who may feel alone or not heard or valued. Kindness like this sends out tidal waves. It's the type of kindness that makes her peers think more critically about what they're typing before hitting the send button.

More than anything, kindness means paying attention to what someone else might need and then doing something about it. My friend Anna's stepdaughter is a shining example of this. Along with the typical angst of being a teenager, she was grieving the death of her father, and the entire family was adjusting emotionally and financially. Somehow, despite all this, she found a way to see beyond her own needs. At sixteen, she had just gotten her first job and couldn't wait to have her own money. The day her stepdaughter received her first paycheck, Anna took her to the bank to set up her account and deposit her check. They were both so proud.

A few days later, Anna received a call from her stepdaughter's teacher. Anna's head spun trying to figure out what was wrong. "Did she forget her uniform? Get sick during class?" But what happened next was a defining moment for Anna and for her stepdaughter—and likely for her teacher, too. The teacher said, "Hello, I'm calling to tell you that your daughter arrived at PE class today with an extra pair of shoes. She had noticed that one of her fellow students didn't have tennis shoes (or much of anything else), and today she very nonchalantly handed him shoes and five pairs of socks. She made sure the other students didn't see her or embarrass the student. But I saw what she did. I kept her after class and asked her about it and she told me she had started her first job. She said she couldn't wait to get her first check so she could give this student some shoes. I thought you should know."

Okay. . . . I'll wait. You go ahead and get that tissue right now. I will be right here wiping my own eyes, too. When I asked Anna how that phone call made her feel, she said, "At a time when our family was struggling, my stepdaughter saw a need she felt was greater and filled it. I was so proud of her. That was ten years ago and her heart continues to grow. She now works in a hospital setting, spreading love and kindness wherever she sees a need."

When you've taught your child compassion, they become attuned to what the people around them may be experiencing and it becomes second nature to look outside their own life and imagine the lives of others. Going a step beyond compassion and moving into action? That's kindness. Anna's stepdaughter is a remarkable example of compassion at work. May her kindness continue to spread to everyone she encounters, beyond anything her mind can comprehend.

FILLING YOUR CUP WITH KINDNESS

Being a mom, wife, entrepreneur, professor, daughter, sister, and friend can sometimes feel overwhelming. The idea of setting aside time just for ourselves is often tainted with shame. Society has told us that taking time for self-care is selfish, and if we are not managing to do it all, then we are less than.

I'll be honest: I am not big on the idea of balancing. I think balance is an illusory state of being that we spend way too much energy chasing. It often leads us down a road of guilt and failure. When we're trying to be all things to all people, we often reach a state of burnout where we end up stuck in a running dialogue of negative self-talk: "I can't believe my house is such a mess." "I feel terrible, I'm stuck in this meeting instead of seeing Johnny at soccer practice." "I'm so mad at myself for skipping the gym again." Your inner mean girl will always let you know when that balance thing isn't working.

I think of my capacity as a teacup. I know that the cup holds a limited amount of liquid and once it reaches its capacity, anything extra overflows onto the saucer and is wasted. Trying to achieve balance is like having a crack in the cup. It allows all the kindness that you pour into yourself to slowly leak out. So how do we begin to turn that around? How do we stop letting that elusive state of balance get in the way of self-care and kindness? We do it with perspective.

I do my best to keep my cup filled with the sweet taste of grace and harmony. Grace, to me, is an act of kindness. Grace allows me to take a break without feeling badly about not being perfect or not being able to be all things to all people. Grace just lets me be. Grace tells me not to worry about the loads of laundry that need to be folded. Grace says, "You deserve to just sit there with your feet up for thirty more minutes doing absolutely nothing." The other ingredient in my cup is a dash of harmony. I try to live my life in a state of harmony, not balance. Let's face it, there are going to be times when you need to focus on a sick child and your work deadline will have to wait. Or you have a huge project at work the night you're supposed to make cupcakes for a school fundraiser. You cannot do both.

When situations like this arise, I ask myself: Where am I needed *most* at this moment? Once I figure that out, I put my energy there and let the other things go. Bestselling novelist Nora Roberts—who's written over two hundred novels—has a great way of explaining this concept. Like all of us, she's got a lot of balls in the air. She says she finds harmony in choosing her priorities by bearing in mind that some of her balls are plastic and some of them are glass. Homemade cupcakes? Those are plastic balls. Big work project? That's a glass ball, so let's not drop that one. Here's what's important to remember: Choosing to do the work project instead of choosing the homemade cupcakes does *not* mean you are prioritizing work over your children. You are prioritizing a big project over cupcakes.

And that's exactly how it should be! Drop that plastic ball, and know that it won't break—you can pick it up again. In fact, in her book *Drop the Ball*, Tiffany Dufu takes this a step further. She asks why women think we have to do it all in the first place and tells us to let go of certain balls that aren't really ours to juggle and not to worry about picking them up again. Ever! Moving with harmony gives us permission not to have to be everything to everyone at the same time. Fewer balls means more time for self-care, which is the only way we'll be the mothers we want to be, mothers who can move through the ebbs and flows of life with grace and patience. I once heard someone say that what you give to everyone around you (partner, children, colleagues, friends, parents, etc.) should be taken from the overflow of your cup (the spillage in the saucer under your teacup) and not what's actually inside. I don't know if I'm there yet, but I'm deciding to at least give myself the first few sips!

This is such important modeling for your kids. When you take the time to recognize that your cup is empty, that you've reached limits that are no longer healthy or sustainable, you model for them the importance of self-awareness and self-care. I use kindness (and grace) for myself when my practices don't align with my core values, or when I know my work is impacting the way I show up for myself and those closest to me. Sometimes my daughter models for me that self-care needs to be added to my schedule, that my cup needs refilling. I love when I FaceTime her while she's away at school and she answers the phone while she is in the bathtub, up to her neck in essential oil-scented bubbles, listening to her music or reading a book. It's a perfect reminder for me to do better and a sweet reminder that I taught her the value in taking time for herself.

Our cups can also be emptied by what is going on in the world around us. When I've taken on so much of the negative energy around me regarding equity and racial injustice, I begin to shut down. I am overwhelmed, and I don't have as much to offer those who need me the most. When the news cycle continues to play images over and over, like the murder of George Floyd, I feel the weight of that on my chest. I still have not watched the video of Floyd's death because I know what that does to me. There is no obligation that says you have to stare at these images or watch these videos. You don't need to check the news all day every day to prove that you are a good and engaged person. Awareness is important, yes. But is checking Twitter going to make you more able to care for yourself and others, or less?

VALUING KINDNESS AT HOME

The 2014 Harvard study *The Children We Mean to Raise* focused on the values that children perceived were most important to their parents. Eighty percent of the children in the study thought their parents valued caring and kindness less than the achievement and happiness of their children. If that statistic hits you in the gut, you're not alone. When I saw it, I wondered whether I had successfully communicated my values to my children, or whether the importance of kindness had gotten lost in all the grades and extracurriculars and homework.

More recently, in 2020, *Parents* magazine conducted its *Parents* values study and surveyed parents across the country on the most important trait they hoped to cultivate in their children. The most popular answer? Kindness. That's encouraging news—but I have to wonder how many parents outwardly express their belief in a certain set of values but communicate (perhaps inadvertently) an opposing set of values in their homes. In the Harvard study, children were also three times more likely to agree that their parents were more proud of them if they got good grades than if they were caring people in their community. It seems our messages of "get straight A's" or "Win this race" are drowning out messages like "Make sure you help someone who needs it" or "Share a smile today." When you review your current parenting, which of these values do you actively and intentionally make the priority to set the foundation for your children's lives?

My good friend Penina has figured this out. Not only does she ignite the flame of kindness in her children—her entire family finds delight in centering kindness as a family activity. As part of their Jewish faith, Penina's family takes part in various mitzvahs, or individual acts of human kindness, in the community. These expressions of kindness include a sense of heartfelt sentiment beyond what is required of oneself. One of my favorite mitzvahs that her entire family has taken part in is the building of the Little Free Pantry.

Like most cities in the country, during the COVID-19 pandemic there was an increase in food insecurity in our area. Through programs at her local synagogue, Penina and her family built their first pantry box for families who were in need. Their inspiration came from the Little Free Libraries in communities where neighbors take and give gently used books. The Little Free Pantry allows community members who are in a financial position to give to place any non-perishable item inside the pantry, and for any person who may need support at any given time to take, without judgment, what they need. The pantry remains open twenty-four hours a day. Over a six-month period, Penina's family has built six Little Free Pantries throughout the city.

When I asked her about the project, she reflected on how her family got started with all of the work that they do in the community. I loved her answer. "Truly, our involvement all began when the boys [her two sons] were preparing for their bar mitzvah and needed volunteer hours at school. We just never stopped. It's because of the kids that we started volunteering as a family." Sometimes if we follow our children's lead, we may end up on a beautiful, life-fulfilling journey that we didn't know we needed. My heart smiles just thinking about the lives that have been touched by my dear friend's family. That's kindness, and it has the power to change the world.

According to studies in neuroscience, children who are kind actually feel happier and more connected to others. When we participate in acts of kindness, we experience a sense of joy. My family has a thing we like to do, and I know we're not alone in it: We pay the bill for the person behind us in line, say at Starbucks or the grocery store. And wow, do my kids get into it! They are so excited, and they try to run out of the store before the person behind us knows we did it. It fills their hearts with joy and, honestly, fills them up with evidence of radical love. How wonderful that we get to be cup fillers for our children!

Marcy and I became great friends after our daughters cemented their friendship in kindergarten. She and her family volunteered to make bookshelves to create a library at a day care facility that supported homeless families with children. During the time that they were working on the library, her youngest daughter had her ninth birthday. One of the gifts Marcy purchased for her daughter was a personalized tool set so she could use it to help build the library. When she opened the gift and saw that it was a set of tools, she looked at her parents incredulously and said, "This is the BEST present I've ever received!" Now how is that for cup filling! Even at nine years old, her daughter knew that gift was one that would keep giving over time. And by the way, that kindness-giving, tool-loving little girl is now a senior in college majoring in engineering! These are the moments that we want sketched on that blueprint. Each time we do this, we build habits of kindness, habits that over time will become permanent.

Social Justice Parenting teaches a lifestyle of kindness, and it can show up in many different ways with many rippling effects, like love rocks in a river. During the year of virtual schooling, I overheard Alexandra on one of her psychology class's Zoom calls telling her professor that giving back was always valued in her house and that she's continued to volunteer at various organizations while she's away at school. She talked about how it helped give her life purpose and how it's been a stepping-stone to who she is and the work she wants to do in the field of psychology. I never mentioned to her that I overheard it, because as my kids get older they don't want to hear all of my "mushy stuff" ("Mom, don't ruin it" or "Mom, that's crunchy"). I've learned to just soak it in, drink it up, fill my cup!

Kindness also fosters a sense of community, as engaging with others helps to create a feeling of belonging. Research shows that this sense of belonging increases levels of the feel-good hormone serotonin and can help reduce depressive symptoms. And the effects are contagious—simply *watching* someone else perform a good deed can increase serotonin. Science proves that kindness has a ripple effect!

The wide-reaching impact of kindness was demonstrated by my dear friend Kalisha and her family, who visited their grandmother in a nursing home during the Christmas season. When they visit, they often sing songs with her. On this occasion, when they started singing, the recreation room began to fill up with other residents, their families, and the staff. Because Kalisha's family are all amazing singers, when they get together it's like being at a concert! Their God-given talents were blessings to the entire nursing home that day. Residents who normally sit in their rooms all day came out swaying to the music or bobbing their heads to the beat. That's a day that will stay in the memory of more people than they intended.

KINDNESS REQUIRES COURAGE

Kindness is not always easy. These stories touch our hearts because we know that being kind isn't always the easy choice. Did my son want to keep the twenty dollars that he found in the park? Probably! Instead, he chose kindness. Choosing kindness offers us a chance to positively impact the life of another human being. That doesn't mean it will always be welcome. Anna's stepdaughter could have inadvertently embarrassed her classmate by giving him a pair of shoes, and her good intentions might have resulted in an unpleasant experience for them both. Extending kindness to others means you take a risk of rejection, judgment, or embarrassment. Courage and kindness are intrinsically linked, and we've all had moments in our lives when we've been glad someone was brave enough to be kind.

My client Ellen, a white woman, confided in me that she wanted to welcome her new neighbor into the community. She would see the neighbor getting in her car, checking the mail, or getting groceries out of the car, but she couldn't get herself to make the introduction. When I pushed her on this fear, she finally admitted that the woman was Black and she was afraid the neighbor would reject her. Maybe they would have nothing to say to each other, or perhaps the neighbor would think she was only being nice because of racial tensions in the country. Ellen was so caught up in her own fears that she was missing an opportunity to be kind to someone. I asked Ellen if she would have these same trepidations if the new neighbor was white. Ellen began to cry. She saw that everything that had been going on in the country following the death of George Floyd had changed her. She realized that in that moment, fear was greater than her kindness. She didn't want this and she definitely didn't want this to be what she was teaching her children.

I finally convinced Ellen to just say hello to her new neighbor the next time she saw her. A few days later, Ellen saw her neighbor retrieving her mail from the mailbox and reluctantly she waved and smiled. The neighbor, Donna, walked across the street, introduced herself, and thanked Ellen for saying hello. After chatting for a while, Ellen realized how her courage was a comfort to Donna, who was in need of Ellen's friendship and welcome to the community. Ellen invited Donna in for coffee and they have been fast-growing friends ever since. Maya Angelou captured it best when she wrote, "Without courage we cannot practice any other virtue with consistency. We can't be kind, true, merciful, generous, or honest." Right now, our country is yearning for those traits to shine through in all of us, just as they did for Ellen that day.

With the assistance from parents and continuous opportunities to practice, children can also develop the skills and courage to know when and how to intervene in circumstances when others need to be lifted up. There are opportunities all around to be a kindness giver and receiver. Some are small but mighty acts, like sharing the last slice of pumpkin pie the day after Thanksgiving (listen, that is a very big deal in my household). Others are more significant with a wider impact, like standing in allyship with Black Lives Matter or with the LGBTQ+ community. You have no way of knowing how your kindness will ripple and grow. Kindness helps you see others in very human ways, the way Ellen did, and it feeds off itself and knocks down walls.

During the height of the racial unrest, many white moms came to me looking for help. They wanted to be allies in the Black Lives Matter movement and they wanted to expand their network so that they included more Black women in their inner circle (a special shout-out to all of my SJP Villagers!). Their intentions were good, but they were making the situation complicated and honestly kind of weird. In trying to understand how to engage more with women of color, one of the moms asked sarcastically, "Do I just go up to her at the store and say hi?" And my reply was, "Yes, that's exactly what you do! Sometimes that kind word is what is needed. Sometimes people just want to be seen. If you just say hello to her, you are letting her know that she *matters*. That's all it takes." You never know what people are going through and how your smile or your hello can change their day.

BUILDING A HABIT OF KINDNESS

Through consistent exposure, all children can develop a habit of kindness. This seems obvious, doesn't it? And yet when I was teaching I would often hear my colleagues refer to their students as "bad" or "those kids" or similar labels. It's disturbing but, unfortunately, all too common. I've seen children unable to live to their fullest potential because an adult didn't take the time to be kind to them. Remember my kindergarten student Rubin? A little time, a little kindness, was all it took. The action that children are exposed to the most is the action that becomes a habit. Learning to be kind is like learning any other skill. My son's coach tells him to shoot one hundred free throws every day. That daily repetition builds that skill, and just like basketball, consistent exposure builds our capacity for care.

A great way to build habits of kindness is through acts of micro-kindness. These are tiny acts of kindness that add up over time. Micro-kindness increases connection in an often disconnected world. Sharing these moments can change a person's attitude in ways that you may never realize and takes little time and effort. These can include things like:

- Complimenting a stranger
- Smiling when you accidentally make eye contact
- Holding the door open for the next person
- Letting someone go in front of you in line
- Saying thank you and using the cashier's name at the grocery store
- Allowing someone to go in ahead of you in traffic
- Saying good morning to the neighbor who never speaks back (I have one of those)

Right now, as a country, we are hurting and hating and we need healing. Healing can only come about when we focus on practicing kindness. The acts of kindness don't have to be grand gestures. They can be small, like a smile. I can't begin to tell you the number of conversations I've had with people just because I smiled at them. My kids don't always get it. They don't understand why I'm always talking to strangers. Sometimes when I smile and say hi to people on the street, my kids say, "Do you know her?" I almost always say no. At which I get, "Oh my gosh, Mom" or eye rolls. And you know what they get from me? You guessed it, a smile. Smiling at others is the simplest act of kindness. It costs you nothing and it benefits everyone.

Anne, one of the women in a coaching program with me, told me a story about her daughter, Payton, who took the idea of a micro-kindness act and multiplied it by five hundred. When her only brother left for college and she was quarantined in the house with her parents, Payton felt the weight of missing her brother. She began to think about other people who may be missing their loved ones, too. She thought about all of the soldiers who were stationed near her hometown. She set a goal of writing five hundred letters to the heroes on the base. This act of kindness demonstrates that you don't need anything fancy to give kindness away. Go ahead, sprinkle that kindness like confetti!

CHAPTER 8

SOCIAL JUSTICE ENGAGEMENT

> Everybody can be great, because everybody can serve.
> You don't have to have a college degree to serve. You
> don't have to make your subject and your verb agree
> to serve. . . . You only need a heart full of grace, a soul
> generated by love.
>
> —Martin Luther King Jr.

It's undeniable that our current sociopolitical environment is unbelievably complex, and its many layers are just plain heavy. I find myself talking to my kids almost daily about issues like equity, race, discrimination, and human dignity. We talk about the necessity of using our voices as agents of change. They know from experience that it isn't always easy to speak out against injustice, but they also know it's the only way to make meaningful change and help create a world where *everyone* feels safe and valued. In fact, young activists have been at the heart of social progress for decades, fighting on the front lines for civil rights and equality. Generation after generation, we've seen how during times of unrest, young leaders are born.

The Children's Crusade of the 1960s civil rights movement is a great example of the power of young activism. When parents were reluctant to march—worried about losing their jobs or being labeled as troublemakers—their children stepped up. At the time, Birmingham was known as one of the most racist cities in the South; in fact, due to the frequent violent attacks on Blacks, it was nicknamed "Bombingham." In May 1963, Dr. Martin Luther King Jr. and the Southern Christian Leadership Conference launched the Children's Crusade, and more than three thousand young Black children left their classrooms in the middle of the day. They marched for three miles from the 16th Street Baptist Church as a protest against segregation and inequality. These children, as young as nine years old, faced great danger, including police dog attacks, being sprayed with fire hoses, and even being arrested and detained in jail. Although they were afraid, their passion and commitment to their cause was greater. They continued to sing their spiritual songs as they were led off to fill the jails for hours, even days at a time. One of the young men of the Children's Crusade remembered Dr. King saying, "I think it's a mighty fine thing for children, what you're doing, because when you march, you're really standing up; because a man can't ride your back unless it is bent."

Within a week after their march, the demands of the children and their parents were met, and slowly, integration began in Birmingham. Many historians believe the success of the Children's Crusade paved the way for Dr. King's famous "I Have a Dream" speech (and his Nobel Peace Prize). So had it not been for the bravery and commitment of these youth activists, the civil rights movement could have been very different. These children were willing to march, to be jailed, to make changes for humanity. Now, all of you bubble parents—you know who you are!—stay with me. I'm not asking you to let your children get arrested, but there's a whole lot of wiggle room between doing nothing and going to jail.

The students at Stoneman Douglas High School in Parkland, Florida, took on their roles as activist leaders in 2018 after the mass shooting in their school. This school is ten miles from my house, and this tragedy was personal. Some of my daughter's travel soccer teammates were students at Stoneman Douglas. I was amazed and awed as I watched these young people step through the fear and into their social activism. Through the tears and the mourning of their friends, the students of Stoneman Douglas High School used their fear to fight back, organize, and create the #NeverAgain movement to demand change for gun control. They stood up to the National Rifle Association on live television and shamed the politicians who had failed to protect them on February 14, 2018. My family took part in our local #NeverAgain march, holding signs, holding hands, and holding on to hope that this would be the last time such violence would happen in our schools. I witnessed how empowered my children felt in that moment, surrounded by other young people fighting for the same cause and having a voice in what their future will look like. And then in 2019, millions of young people across the globe raised their voices in mass protests, demanding action to reverse the climate crisis.

More recently, we witnessed the bravery of the thousands of young people of all racial, ethnic, and socioeconomic backgrounds who gathered together peacefully to stand with the Black community after the murder of George Floyd. These young adults filled the streets in every major city across the country. *USA Today* reported protesters in more than 580 cities (big, small, urban, and rural) as thousands of people stood up against the systemic racism that has plagued the Black community. This reckoning on live television helped many see that this is not just a Black problem—it's everyone's problem. The raised voices of young people remind the rest of us that their future depends on the decisions we are making now. They aren't going to sit around and wait for us to do the right thing. They see the need to be truth tellers and change makers. They are reflecting, resisting, and rallying. And we, as the adults in their lives, have to be strong enough to support them or smart enough to get out of their way.

RAISING JUSTICE-MINDED KIDS

In its simplest form, social justice is about human rights. It's about improving the lives of all historically marginalized groups, based on race, ethnicity, nationality, gender, sexual orientation, age, religion, disability, and more. Social justice is about distributing power so everyone has a fair chance to live a full, productive life. It is something we should all be able to agree on.

Engaging in acts of social justice means doing your part to ensure that all groups of people have access to opportunities for growth (like education), opportunities for equity in resources (like food and affordable housing), opportunities for participation (like voting and employment), and opportunities for basic rights (like safety, fair legal representation, and health care). As parents, we want our children not only to benefit from these rights but to champion access for all individuals. The ultimate goal of Social Justice Parenting is to raise children who can self-advocate, empathize with others, and be proactive in stopping injustices. Remember, when we create safe places of belonging in our home, our children will grow up to create spaces of belonging in the world. It is up to us to guide them so that standing up for others and speaking out against inequity are simply viewed as normal behavior—this is just *what we do.*

In order to facilitate this mindset in your children, you need to show them how it's done—literally. The more you model intellectually curious behaviors, including pushing back against the status quo when it comes to the issues that are most important to you, the more these habits of activism will be normalized. If we show our children how to respond to injustices, whether that's spreading awareness and volunteering or taking part in marches and boycotts, they will develop their own sense of social justice engagement. If you haven't prioritized your core values, and if they don't guide your own choices and actions, your children are unlikely to make social activism a regular part of their lives.

In my work with families, I challenge them to find something that they are all passionate about. It could be creating a community food pantry or donating resources to a local women's shelter. Honestly, there's a *lot* of injustice in the world, so surely you can find something you want to focus on. It doesn't matter where you choose to start; the point is to identify something that moves you and do something about it. You are teaching your children that caring is only the beginning. It's not enough to stop there—they must take action to make change happen.

Our role as adults is to guide our children at all ages as they navigate their natural inquisitiveness and curiosity in ways that expand their knowledge and their love for others. Social justice engagement is the intentional practice of addressing human rights issues, locally and globally. Everyone can do this. Everyone *should* do this! It is the pathway to becoming an architect of change.

When children see someone struggling or being treated unfairly, their inclination is to help. Sharing their toys, helping someone who has fallen down—these are natural behaviors that occur one on one. This is kindness, a.k.a. compassion in action, and it should absolutely be encouraged! But true social justice engagement goes beyond the individual, moving to the root cause of issues like homelessness, poverty, or the mistreatment of immigrants. Rather than just looking at individuals who have needs, social justice engagement takes a step back to look at the systemic factors that are affecting groups of people. Examples of acts of social justice engagement include talking to lawmakers to ensure they provide affordable housing for everyone, calling on employers to treat employees fairly, or working to make sure your schools have proper resources to educate all students. Your responsibility is to find a bridge between kindness and social justice engagement—and that bridge is activism.

When you think about activism, you may imagine unrest, violence, or the presence of law enforcement. We've definitely seen our fair share of that in the last couple of years! But activism can look different for different people. There is no wrong way to be an activist, as long as you are taking positive steps toward actionable change. Explain to your children, "Activism is the act of bringing attention or awareness to issues or topics that you feel passionately about in hopes of bringing about change. Your passion is something that you feel strongly about; something you know really needs to change and that you want to change for the better. That's where your activism can start." Activism is a way for your kids to learn important life lessons while doing good in the world. It allows them to channel their passion for a topic to raise awareness and bring about change. When I give my children a global lens through which to see the world, I know they're able to recognize their own privilege. Just like for us adults, thinking about the world's problems can lead to despair and a sense of helplessness. But activism is the antidote to despair. Activism gives children purpose and drive. It's an answer to their need for belonging, as it gives them a chance to build a community with others who share the same passion. It teaches them how to work together with a diverse group of people. This kind of involvement teaches them the skill of supporting others and the art of knowing when to stand your ground and when to compromise. As the late Supreme Court justice Ruth Bader Ginsburg memorably said, "Fight for the things that you care about, but do it in a way that will lead others to join you."

KID-FRIENDLY ACTIVISM

There is *so much* your kids can do to create positive change in the world, and activism empowers children to use their voices to educate others (including their parents) on topics that are important to them. They develop skills in planning, problem solving, persuading, and public speaking—all life skills that we want our children to be able to tap into as they become adults.

There's no one right way to be an activist. Think broadly about the way you define activism, and consider how you and your kids can best use your skills to support others. Sometimes it's marching, protesting, or being loud, but sometimes it's more of a quiet passion, working behind the scenes to help others and ourselves (you can't take care of others if you don't take care of yourself). Activism is about taking action. Your parenting, let me remind you, is a form of activism where you are actively raising children who are change makers in the world.

For the purposes of our discussion, I've organized various forms of activities into two categories. It is not a hierarchical list but is based on the time, energy, and effort that are needed in the engagement. Please remember, there is a great need for activism on all levels. No act is too small. Alice Walker reminds us that "activism is [our] rent for living on the planet." Every good that you do sends positive vibrations out into the world. Imagine raising the globe's vibrations so high that we all can feel it shake.

Category I

Volunteering. Volunteering typically involves helping to meet people's immediate individual needs on a short-term basis. This includes most of the activities we think about as "community service" or "giving back," like donating food to a food bank, serving at a homeless shelter, tutoring children, or assisting a refugee family. These are all examples of volunteer work. When you model this type of activism, make sure you put the focus on helping humankind, not giving to the "needy" or the "poor." Let children know we all need help sometimes and it's more about selfless giving and less about the power dynamic of the haves and have-nots. Many of you may have a habit of charitable giving during the holiday season. My girlfriend Yolanda and her daughters invite friends over to have bag-stuffing parties where they pack bags of food for families in need during the Thanksgiving season. This is a great way to show your children that they're helping other kids who aren't that different from them.

Oftentimes the act of volunteering or giving is a bit distanced, as we put food on the shelves at a pantry or donate clothes to a shelter. It's important to emphasize that these are real people that you're helping. This will help your kids recognize their impact.

Awareness/Consciousness-Raising. I have an activity I do in one of my multicultural undergraduate courses at the university. When we are discussing LGBTQ+ issues in schools and the role of the teacher in creating safe spaces for their students, I ask each of my students to choose a round metal button pin from my basket. When they choose a button, they have no idea what it says or why they have to wear it. They are instructed to get a classmate to pin the button on them and not look down at it. In the basket are four types of buttons with

one of the following words printed on them: Straight, Gay, Nonconforming, LGBTQ+ Ally. I go through the rest of the class teaching
my lesson, engaging with the students around that session's content.
By the end of class time, most of the students forget that they are
wearing the buttons. As the students begin to leave the classroom
I stand at the front door with my basket and tell them they can either keep and wear their button outside (again, not knowing what
their button says) or they can take it off and hand it to me as they
leave.

I've been doing this exercise for ten years, and let me tell you—
ten years ago, I got most of my buttons back. No one wanted to
risk accidentally wearing a button that misidentified them. But these
days I have to replenish my basket of buttons after each semester.
The shift in young people's acceptance and willingness to support
others who are different from them continues to grow. The students
wear the buttons as visual representations of their support. I can
recall walking across campus hours later after teaching that lesson and seeing a couple of my students in the line at Starbucks still
wearing their buttons. They were jumping up and down, waving to
me, pointing to their buttons. I went over and high-fived them and
smiled.

I even had one student, who was wearing the LGBTQ+ Ally
button, send me an email the next day to let me know that the lesson
had changed her. She was approached by someone in the LGBTQ+
community in the parking lot who saw her pin and came up to her
to say that he was having a rough day and her pin let him know he
was not alone and he thanked her. That button became a permanent
part of her backpack. I would see it pinned in the middle of the front
pocket of her bag every day she came into my class for the rest of the
semester.

Pins like this—along with ribbons, bumper stickers, and other tokens of support—are one way to show your allegiance to a cause. Another common form of activism is participating in an organized march, run, ride, or walk for a specific cause. Cooper, my energetic, beautiful, and assertive niece, has Down syndrome, and each year my extended family joins the thousands of other families who participate in the Buddy Walk. We are the loud and crazy family who proudly hold the banner displaying COOPER'S TROOPERS. It's a great opportunity for all of us to spend the day together and to get to know other families who share a common goal or interest. And, of course, it's another way to teach our children empathy and kindness. Find a walk that inspires your family, and know that each step is a statement of your willingness to support the organization and the people and causes behind it.

Internet Activism. Our communities online can be just as powerful as our communities in person. While internet activism is sometimes dismissed as the "easiest" form of activism—how much effort does it take to click "repost," after all?—it can also be surprisingly effective. If you have a wide platform of friends and relatives who don't necessarily agree with your views, Facebook can be a great way to raise awareness, counter misinformation, and make space for underrepresented voices. According to Pew Research, around 80 percent of Black people believe that social media can help magnify issues that are rarely discussed elsewhere. Consider the case of George Floyd, for instance: His death was not reported in traditional news media until the video of the incident had already gone viral on social media. How many of us would never have known what happened if there had not been internet activism around this issue? Internet activism may be quick and easy, but it can spark more awareness, and thus higher levels of participation.

That said, there are some inherent challenges with internet activism. One is making sure that the information you're sharing (or viewing) is accurate. There's a lot of distortion and misinformation out there, on both sides of the political spectrum, and so it's important to check your sources and only post from reputable ones. If your children are old enough to be on social media themselves, make sure you've taught them good fact-checking habits. (Snopes.com is a great resource.)

Another challenge with social media activism is ensuring that you're reaching beyond your bubble. Social media can often turn into an echo chamber of everyone shouting at the people they already agree with. This changes no one's mind and therefore isn't particularly effective as a form of activism. Finally, I encourage you to model for your children *engagement* on social media rather than ranting. As tempting as it can be to rage-tweet—a temptation I have certainly felt myself!—posting something in a moment of anger, even if it is justified, will not spark a discussion and could actually cause damage. When I am feeling passionate about a topic, I often choose to educate and provide resources in a post, with the intention to create critical dialogue. Calling back to our beloved Notorious RBG, remember to fight for the things you care about in a way that will bring other people to the fight, too.

Category II

Letter Writing & Petitions. What issues are you most concerned about? What rules/laws are unfair to specific groups of people? Is there anything going on in your neighborhood or community that needs the attention of lawmakers? Perhaps there are issues in your state or the country that are bothering you. Whatever you choose to focus on, work together with your family to write a letter to a person who can help you make changes in your local community.

This person could be the school principal or it could be a politician. In your letter, explain what your concern is and why it's an issue for you and/or your family. You should also include a couple of possible solutions. In your letter, thank them in advance for taking the time to read your letter and their consideration in addressing your concerns. Remember to ask them to confirm that they received it.

Demonstrations. A demonstration is a gathering of a large group of people for a common cause. It's a way to connect with other people who share a viewpoint on an issue and bring attention to that issue. Demonstrations can take the form of rallies, marches, sit-ins, and strikes. This form of activism has a long and rich history. Think about the Protestant Reformation in the 1500s—that was a protest movement with demonstrations. The Boston Tea Party was a demonstration against unfair taxation. Dr. Martin Luther King Jr.'s March on Washington is credited with being the force behind President Kennedy's push for civil rights legislation.

This kind of activism can have an enormous impact. There is always a chance for violence to erupt—and not every demonstration is appropriate for children. But there is a way to participate safely, and being a part of an enormous crowd of protesters can make you feel part of a community of change, giving you a sense of belonging and power. That's exactly what we want for our children.

Boycott. A boycott is when groups of people refuse to buy products or services from a company or organization. Again, it can seem like a small action—just "don't buy this product"—but boycotts have the power to effect meaningful change. You'll likely have heard of the Montgomery Bus Boycott during the civil rights movement, which started with Rosa Parks and led to the outlaw of segregation on public buses. The Delano Grape Strike led by César Chávez brought about the formation of the first farm labor union. The boycott of SeaWorld forced the company to stop their abuses against orcas. As an individual, it may not always feel like you can make much of a difference, but you never know what big waves your small ripples can grow into. The boycott of Chick-fil-A in 2012, for instance, didn't appear to impact its sales much because there weren't *that* many people participating, but the publicity around the boycott created "reputational harm"—and that caused the company to stop donating to anti-LGBTQ+ organizations.

Organizing and participating in a boycott is a way to force social change by hitting companies where it hurts. It's something you can easily get your kids involved in, and when it's something they really don't want to give up, it can teach them how important it is for your actions and purchases to align with your values.

GETTING STARTED

When your children grow up watching you take action in your community—and better yet, participating in that action with you—they'll develop social justice engagement muscles that will last a lifetime. Let's face it: Children are already exposed to social issues, through the media, through their friends, through school, or through adult conversations that they overhear. Addressing complicated issues at home gives you the chance to answer questions and provide accurate information so that you can take responsible action together.

Start with a passion project. If you aren't sure what issues your family members are passionate about, use the table below to brainstorm. Think about how you as a family can use those passions to make your community a better place. The first column has been filled to provide you with examples.

EXAMPLE FAMILY MEMBER— WHAT ARE MY PASSIONS?	FAMILY MEMBER #1 WHAT ARE MY PASSIONS?	FAMILY MEMBER #2 WHAT ARE MY PASSIONS?	FAMILY MEMBER #3 WHAT ARE MY PASSIONS?	FAMILY MEMBER #4 WHAT ARE MY PASSIONS?
I want to help homeless people.				
I want to help manatees because they are endangered.				
I want to close the educational gap for people of color.				

As a family, decide which passion you will work on first. Then discuss what your family can do, within both Category I activism and Category II activism. Use the example below, which focuses on helping people who are homeless, to spark a discussion about actions your family can take.

EXAMPLES OF CATEGORY I ACTIVISM	EXAMPLES OF CATEGORY II ACTIVISM
We can donate canned goods to a local charity for Thanksgiving dinner.	We can write letters to our local representative to provide more housing options for families without shelters in the community.
When we see a panhandler on the side of the road, we can give them a dollar.	We can organize a mitten, blanket, and sock drive to draw media attention to the lack of available shelters in the city for people who are homeless.

Your next step is to educate yourself on the topic and to decide as a family what your goals are. What are you hoping to accomplish? List your short, immediate goals as well as your long-term goals to keep you motivated and organized around your passions. Create visuals like posters, vision boards, or even Post-it Notes, so that your children will see the difference your family is making. These visuals will help you stay on track while you're implementing your action plan. The world needs you, and the world needs you to raise children who believe that they can make a difference by using their power and their voices for good.

CHAPTER 9

MODELING ADVOCACY

I learned a long time ago the wisest thing I can do is be on
my own side, be an advocate for myself and others like me.
—Maya Angelou

We've talked a lot about teaching our children the importance of being compassionate and using their privilege to advocate for others. These qualities empower the next generation to help create a better world for us all. But as important as it is for your children to be allies and change agents, it's equally critical that they learn how to ask for what they need. It's never too early—or too late—to start teaching your children about self-advocacy.

As parents, it's sometimes easier (and less messy) to do everything for our children. We monitor how long it's been since they've had a drink of water or a snack. We check their homework to make sure it's correct. We're afraid to let them make mistakes. Monitoring our kids so closely may solve their problems in the short term, but it doesn't set them up for long-term success. In order to do that, we need to nurture skills that will support independent goal setting and action. We need to instill the ability to make good choices and find people who will help support them when we're not present to advocate on their behalf.

Encouraging this kind of independence isn't always easy. Let's face it: There are times when we bail out our children not because we think it's best for them but because we worry about how their mistakes would make us look as parents or how their mistakes might damage our family's reputation. It's hard to shake the impulse to be a mama bear, someone who is always there to rescue her cubs. I get it. I can't even begin to tell you how many last-minute Hobby Lobby or Michaels runs I've done when I couldn't bear to let my kid turn in a less-than-Martha-Stewart-ready project because of how it would make *me* look. I have done midday homework runs, after-school sneakers drop-offs, and last-minute pickups (because let's get real, my kids will not call their dad for these items). I have replaced lost items like books (I swear our local library should name a wing after me— I'm sure my late-fee payments could build it!). I've even replaced cell phones that were left on the train or dropped in the bathtub. I have cleaned up their messes. But the thing is, when you're always running around fixing their issues or catering to their needs, they never get the chance to develop problem-solving or decision-making skills.

Over the years, I realized that I was doing a disservice to my children by taking care of all their problems. I knew I had to find harmony in being there for them and supporting their needs while also teaching them to support themselves when I wasn't around. I realized that the earlier our children begin to find ways to speak up for themselves, the better and more comfortable they will be when they really need to use this skill. I had to make a big leap from the mother I was when my older kids were in elementary school—the annoyed, sometimes overinvolved parent who didn't let her child address the issue before jumping in—to the mother I am now. Today I sit on my hands, waiting with bated breath, to see how my kids will handle a situation, jumping in only if it's strictly necessary. I am a work in progress, and seeing my children struggle is difficult. But I know that struggling now, while having me as a safety net or soft place to land, is necessary for their growth. It scaffolds their journey to self-advocacy.

SELF-ADVOCACY

Self-advocacy is the act of expressing your personal needs (mental, physical, or emotional) in hopes of getting them met. It includes knowing your rights and responsibilities, gathering information to make decisions for your life, and then using that information to surround yourself with a group of people who support your journey in navigating in the world. It includes making knowledgeable choices and taking responsibility for those choices. Many studies have suggested that children who are taught self-advocacy skills have an increased likelihood of becoming happy, well-adjusted adults.

Self-advocacy is an important skill that can help children create solutions in their lives, including in school, with family and peers, in relationships, and in the community. Learning to become an effective self-advocate is all about educating the people around you on how to treat you, and the expectations that you have for yourself and for the way you want to be valued. It's about asking for help, something we all need at times. It may be difficult for your children (and for you), but with continuous modeling, practicing, and consistency, this skill will develop over time. And honestly? It frees you up to focus on other things (like deciding what the heck you're cooking for dinner every day). I also encourage (more like require) my children to speak up to their teachers when they have questions or when they think their assignment wasn't graded fairly. When they draft the email, I will look it over and give them feedback before they hit send, and with practice they've grown better at presenting calm, nondefensive perspectives. The more successes they have with these small tasks, the more comfortable they will feel tackling the hard stuff as adults, like asking for a raise or pushing back against an abusive boss. Like anything else, the more you engage in something, the better you understand it and the easier it gets.

Whether you're an adult or a kid, self-advocacy is a vital skill. There's no way to get what you want if you don't communicate what you need. Think about your one-year-old who isn't verbal yet. The best way to get you to know what they want is to cry, so they cry when they're tired, when they're hungry, when they're wet. They cry when they're hurt. Eventually, you learn to decipher the differences among the cries, but imagine how much easier it would be if your toddler could just say, "Mom, I'm feeling tired right now. Could you snuggle with me for a few minutes, then put me in my crib so I can go to sleep?" It would take the guesswork out of the situation for you, and it would make them feel pretty good about asking for what they need and getting it. The moment your children become verbal is the time to begin teaching self-advocacy skills. If you have older children and you haven't started yet, that's okay! You can begin right now.

Self-advocacy looks different depending on the age and even the personality of your child. For example, Rachel, the host of *3 in 30 Podcast for Moms*, spoke to me about trying to teach her daughter, seven at the time, who is an introvert, how to self-advocate. She used the word "yet" when describing the self-advocacy skill her daughter was trying to master. Rachel discussed talking to a group of moms at a playdate about her child. "She's still learning how to use her voice. She's not mastered this skill *yet*." No one knows your child better than you. Your approach should be based on their personality and learning style.

Regardless of how and when they develop these skills, the ability to self-advocate increases a child's self-confidence and self-reliance. Wouldn't it be fantastic to know that your children feel like they can control their own destiny? That they feel confident in their decision making and ability to take on life's challenges? When your kids grow up in a home where they know their ideas and concerns matter and they're given the space to figure things out on their own, they'll take that sense of value and agency out into the world. And when occasions arise where they need to speak up—either for themselves or for others—they will.

THE THREE STEPS OF SELF-ADVOCACY

The journey of self-advocacy is an ongoing process, but it can be helpful to think about it in three parts: knowing yourself, naming your needs, and articulating what and who is required to get those needs met. It's important that we teach our kids that their needs matter and that it's okay to take up space and time.

Know Yourself

Self-knowledge is the first step to self-advocacy, and spending time getting to really know your children will help them know their own strengths, as well as the areas where they need support. After my children's sporting events, I always encourage them to reflect on their performances. I ask them to tell me how they thought they played. "What did you do well today during the game? What made you proud of your performance today?" I want to give them an opportunity to engage in self-reflection, to feel comfortable seeing their hard work and successes in a positive light, rather than experiencing it as "bragging" or something negative. Then I ask them, "What could you have done better/differently? What do you want to work on at practice next week?" Their answers to these questions help me assess how well my children can self-regulate, how well they can monitor and manage their emotions, thoughts, and behaviors. I need to see that they can constructively analyze their actions, identifying opportunities for improvement without feeling ashamed or getting stuck in negative thinking. These conversations also help me see what my kids need from me. It supports my core value of creating a community of belonging in my home.

Helping your child discover their strengths and challenges allows them to get to know who they are. Before they can self-advocate, they have to know themselves. They have to know what's important to them, they have to understand how to give and receive information, and they have to be aware of their individual learning styles. My son and I spent time developing a curricular unit around what ADHD was and what his body needed to support him. This knowledge helped him to regulate some of his own actions and, in turn, to tell his teachers and other adults what he needed.

Self-awareness, including understanding your strengths and challenges and knowing what helps you thrive, is the first step to self-advocacy. I would suggest creating family time dedicated to this activity. Every year on New Year's Day, my family and I engage in activities that support our efforts to recommit to our goals and what we need to do to make sure they are actualized. One of the activities is each person having a word-of-the-year. A few of our words in the past year included "abundance," "strength," and "love." We each add our word on one of the walls in our family room as a reminder of our goals and to support our manifesting and visualizing. We also each create a vision board for the upcoming year. I put out stickers, magazines, markers, and construction paper and we all work together discussing what images, quotes, and symbols that we are putting on our boards and why. We then write our upcoming academic/career goals, personal goals, and family goals. We also write our three greatest strengths that will lead us to success with these goals, try to predict possible roadblocks, and figure out the resources (including human) that will support us in reaching these goals. Over the course of the year, we try to remind each other of those goals, and then at the end of the year, we revisit them. Did we achieve our goals? Or do they need to be tweaked and added to next year's list? Regardless of whether or not we achieved everything we'd hoped, we remind each other of our small successes and celebrate our progress.

Other fun ways to really get to know your children could include: reserving one-on-one dates where your child gets to plan the agenda; pen pal journaling, the way my son and I shared a journal back and forth as a way to communicate our deep feelings; a family questions jar, a mason jar with questions written on Popsicle sticks pulled during dinnertime; the question of the week, handwritten on a whiteboard in a high-traffic space in your home for family members to answer throughout the week; and "what would you do" scenarios during dinner or while driving around, which can help you get a pulse on your children's thinking and problem-solving skills.

Another activity that you can do with your children is an inventory. It serves as a cheat sheet for you to know your children and as a tool for your children to articulate what they need. This inventory is a way to get at who your child is and what they need to be successful. Ideas for starter questions can include:

- The areas that I am strong in are . . .
- The things that I struggle with are . . .
- Here's what I wish people really understood about me . . .
- I feel most stressed when . . .
- I feel the most at peace when . . .
- When I need help, I usually . . .

Understanding your child—the way they give and receive information, the way they express joy and fear—is vital to helping them understand themselves on their personal journey of self-advocacy.

Articulating Your Needs

After reflecting on their goals and needs, the next step in self-advocacy is articulating those needs to others. In order to teach this idea, you must model it. Through your own authentic interactions with others, you model what genuinely listening to and respecting others' opinions and advice looks like, as well as how to evaluate decisions. Ultimately we want to teach our children to trust their intuition, to home in to that nagging awareness in their gut that something is or isn't right. I always tell my children, if your head and your gut are not aligned, go with what your gut is telling you.

Modeling self-advocacy involves being active and mindful of your own internal cues. I try to model this in my children's lives when the stakes are low or when the process of making a decision is not a very stressful one (I tend to make big decisions on my own, rather than using them as teaching moments). For example, if we're out somewhere and things aren't going as expected, I use the "think aloud" strategies that I've modeled for so many years as an educator. If we're at a restaurant and the waiter brings me food that's not quite what I ordered, I'll talk through the thought process of deciding if I want to say something or just be okay with eating what was brought to me. The think-aloud would sound something like this: "I asked them not to put the cheese on my salad but I see that my salad is covered with cheese. I could just forget about it and eat it or I could ask them to remake my salad as I asked for it since I am paying for the service. Is it worth waiting another ten minutes to get a new one? I think I'm going to speak up and say something because I won't enjoy my dinner as much the way it is right now."

This kind of modeling in the small moments helps build your children's self-advocacy for the big moments. I require my children to ask for the things they might ordinarily let go, like some extra sauce or more napkins. I won't do it for them; they have to speak up for themselves. I encourage my sons to advocate for themselves when getting their haircuts: "I would like it shorter on the sides. Can you please cut more off?"

When my oldest son wanted to run for student council president, some of his friends tried to convince him to run for vice president instead. A friend of his was also running for president, and people in his circle were suggesting that he couldn't win and that he should settle for VP. When he told me about the decision he was trying to make, I asked him, "Do you want to be president? If so, you know what to do." That simple question and statement was all he needed. He decided that he had just as good a shot as anyone else. He spent weeks advocating for himself to convince fellow classmates (and himself) that he would be a good president. Seems simple for us as adults, but it is a skill that has to be nurtured and reinforced. Children are insightful; they internalize what we do and how we feel. The more they see advocating as a part of our interaction with others, the more automatic it becomes for them. And yes, he became the student council president in his senior year of high school.

Teaching your children to explore resources and articulate their needs is the ultimate goal of self-advocating. We want our kids to know that asking for support is a sign of strength, not weakness. Asking for support is a way that we evolve and grow as human beings. Guiding your children in the way they ask questions and speak to adults can lead to more effective communication, a skill that is unfortunately eroding these days with the continued increase of technology-based communication. Our children do not use the beauty and complexity of language in the ways that support them in asking others for what they need. Often, they just don't know what to say.

When you model your core values, you fortify your child's ability to connect with others in an effective way and, therefore, their capability to be confident and articulate communicators. Finding the balance between being assertive and not aggressive is an art, and it cannot be taken for granted. I always tell my children it isn't what you say but how you say it. In a world where people are doing more talking *at* people or *over* people, it gets noisy, and, honestly, sometimes it gets scary. I think about the division in our country and the camps that we find ourselves in because no one is talking in ways that the other side wants to (or can) hear. How can anyone expect to get their needs met if they're presented in a manner that puts the other person on the defensive? Teaching your children to be clear, thoughtful, and flexible—without conceding their most important needs—is a complicated dance that takes experience and practice. I try to teach my children to come up with a plan of action instead of just a list of complaints.

During the pandemic, my youngest son was not adjusting well to virtual school. The transition from brick-and-mortar elementary school to virtual middle school was overwhelming. Because I was managing my own pandemic-induced stress, I didn't notice he was struggling until the midterm grades came out. I had done all the things—bought the new Chromebook, bought the new desk and chair, invested in high-speed internet, prepared breakfast and lunch every day, and asked "How's it going? Everything turned in?" But looking back, I never really checked in. I assumed he was doing fine, just as he always had in elementary school.

I have to admit, at first I was very angry when I saw his grades. How could he possibly be doing so poorly when I was running around serving him and his siblings all day so all of their needs were met and all he had to do was to show up for class? But what he really needed was *me*. He needed me to take a minute to slow down and support him, to show him how to manage six classes with six different teachers, who all want different things from him. He needed me, not all "the things." And so we sat down with his list of needs that he articulated to me. We moved his desk from his bedroom to my office space with me. We set up his binders and talked about note taking. We set up his whiteboard so he could immediately write his color-coded daily assignments for each class. And he got back on track.

Build Your Village

The last step in self-advocacy is knowing who to go to for support. Building a village where you can be vulnerable and nurtured is a life-long skill. And unfortunately it's one that we often need to work on because we're still recovering from negative and sometimes hurtful past experiences. In her book *Rising Strong*, Brené Brown talks about the importance of setting clear boundaries. Boundaries give our children (and us) a sense of agency. They allow us to have some control over the people and situations that we choose to make a part of our supportive village. I know I've been there. I've had that friend who was *always* in a crisis, who always needed help . . . but was never really there for me when I needed support. I think we've all experienced that at one time or another. We've all been in relationships that haven't felt supportive. And we've also all known what it's like to truly feel like someone has your back, that they will hold us and pick us up when we fall. Those people make up your village.

You don't have to make yourself available to everyone—it's okay to say no. In fact, it's crucial. Often we don't listen to our instincts, our gut reactions, because we are taught to be polite, or we second-guess our biological response. We teach our children, especially our girls, to be nice and polite and not to hurt others' feelings, without teaching the flip side of that, which is to create and enforce boundaries around what is acceptable to you and what is not. You can't be vulnerable or supported when someone crosses your clearly defined boundaries. My daughter has stayed in toxic friendships because she felt she needed to "save" someone or "be there" for them, or because she was afraid of having to end a friendship and find new friends. As much as I wanted to save her from these heartaches, I knew she had to go through them. It's the only way she could really identify her deal breakers and learn to create some boundaries. Teach your children to focus on the red flags in relationships that make them feel uncomfortable or unsafe. Talk about these feelings openly so children will know it's okay to have them and it doesn't make them a bad person, and it doesn't make them any less nice.

You can teach your child how to be self-aware and self-reflective by ensuring they're able to identify and name what they're feeling. Once they're able to identify their big emotions, they'll be able to ask for support or speak up for what they need in various situations. During his middle school years, my oldest son was struggling with anxiety, and he worked extensively on developing coping mechanisms. I knew we needed to create a supportive village that could be there for him when I couldn't. I sat down with him and told him that we needed to work out a plan so that he would have what he needed to stay calm and focused throughout the day. We started by creating a list of the adults at his school whom he thought would be good "team members" for him, including his guidance counselor, a couple of his teachers, the assistant principal, and his theater coach. We then looked at each of the adults on the list and brainstormed what their roles could be in supporting him. We set up a meeting with the team to articulate his needs and share how we would like each person to support him, as well as how he could communicate if he was in a crisis and needed immediate attention.

After the meeting, the assistant principal, who had a close family member who suffered from anxiety and who was incredibly supportive of my son, came up with a "Willy Wonka golden ticket" system.

She would give my son three golden tickets per trimester. These could be used only when his anxiety was so high that he couldn't wait to talk about it with his teachers. He would just get his teacher's attention and present the golden ticket. The teacher would excuse him from the classroom and he would report right to the assistant principal's office, and she could help bring his anxiety levels down. Her office was his safe space, and when she wasn't too busy, she would even meet with him to work on understanding the sources of his anxiety and help him develop coping skills to manage it.

You can use this example as a way to navigate any situation where your child will have to make decisions that impact aspects of their lives, including sports, performances, or family events that may or may not involve you. Self-education, effective communication, and maintaining a support system are the keys to becoming an effective self-advocate. To make sure that your children are comfortable with making a plan and recruiting support, you can role-play difficult situations so they will have the language and the strategies they need to make an empowered ask. Once your child has become proficient at role playing, you can put your children in low-stakes situations where they're practicing some of these skills—for instance, you can encourage your child to place their own order in a restaurant, to return an item to a store, or to talk to their teacher about a particular assignment or grade. This requires them to practice being assertive yet respectful.

HELPING CHILDREN SELF-ADVOCATE

One mistake made by many well-meaning parents—including me—is telling children how they feel or how they should feel. For example, a child might say, "I don't like strawberries" and the parent replies, "Yes you do, you used to eat them all the time when you were little." When my son falls during driveway basketball and tells my husband he's hurt, like many fathers, my husband often responds, "You're not hurt" or "That didn't hurt that bad." The only way children will learn to ask for what they need from others is to know how to name what they are feeling, and know that they will be heard and believed. Creating opportunities to be independent and to praise their efforts for speaking up are necessary components of self-advocacy. You can't ask for help when you're being denied your own emotions. The more you give your children opportunities to connect to their intuition and speak on it, without having to overexplain, rationalize, or defend their thoughts and feelings, the better they will be able to remain confident and unwavering in asking for what they need. This creates independence and eventually leads to the skill of advocating for themselves.

Being able to ask for help is a skill worth openly acknowledging and rewarding. When a child can openly express when they are worried, have a fear, or have a specific need, take time to let them know how proud you are of them for being able to identify that need and speak up. These issues could be as small as your child's fear that during school they might not be able to unbutton and rebutton their pants to use the bathroom, to your child feeling anxious about saying no when their peers ask them to drink at a high school party. When a problem comes up, give your child a chance to solve it before stepping in to fix it for them. Give them space to problem-solve and figure out their options. They might well determine that they can solve it without your help. When you encourage them to problem-solve at home, they will feel more empowered to do so in other environments. I know it's easier to do it yourself. I know it's painful to watch them struggle. I know it's hard to watch when you know they aren't necessarily making the best decision. Trust me: been there, done that! But I promise you this: It will be so worthwhile in the long run. Allowing them to struggle for a little bit, and only stepping in when you are *truly* needed, is what will help them grow into confident advocates for themselves and others.

Collaborative problem solving, like the strategizing I did with my oldest son, can be a good way for both you and your child to practice self-advocacy. Once you brainstorm and identify the best solution, you can work with your child on figuring out the steps to get to that solution. This teaches both cooperation and self-advocacy through recognizing problems and the capacity to make changes happen. It also shows them that their thoughts and opinions matter. Even for children who seem confident and assertive in many areas, lessons in self-advocacy help them to effectively express their needs in areas where they may feel less confident. Self-advocacy doesn't mean doing it all alone. It means knowing when and how to ask for help, and who can provide that support.

CONCLUSION

None of this is going to be easy. I mean, let's face it, parenting isn't easy, and throwing in the additional labor of parenting for social justice can sometimes feel like the straw that's going to break your back. It's easy to see it as one more thing to do, one more thing to stress about. "I know I need to do something but I just don't know how." "Am I doing it right?" "Can my family really change anything?"

There are plenty of times when I question whether it's all worth it, whether my voice and my guidance are enough to drown out the negative messages my kids are receiving elsewhere, and whether enough other moms are raising their kids to be anti-racists and compassionate to make a real change in the world. Will any of it make a difference?

One thing that I know for certain: I don't want to leave it up to others to teach my children the values that are the foundation of the work that I do. We all have moments of struggle. That's what makes the mosaic of moms so powerful. We need to lean on each other when moments like Breonna Taylor and George Floyd's deaths make it hard to for us to breathe, let alone talk to our kids. These are the times when we can lean into our collective power to create belonging in the world. If we really think about it, these are the times when we recognize that social justice doesn't just happen; we need to do the work within our families to change the narrative and make it happen. Motherhood *is* activism.

And then I'll have a moment, an inspiring, motivating moment, that will give me the strength to keep going. I'll watch my son offer to play with the trans kid on the playground, or extend a hand to help a differently abled child. I'll watch my daughter show up with a "strong back and soft front" in response to a sexist comment one of her classmates made. And I'll see someone else's son or daughter stand up for my children in return.

Remember how you felt when you heard Amanda Gorman, our nation's first-ever youth poet laureate, recite her inauguration poem on January 20, 2021? I immediately thought about my children when Amanda challenged us to leave the world better than how it was when we inherited it. We can do that using the tools of Social Justice Parenting.

As I took in the magic of every word she so gracefully uttered on that historical day, I felt the collective exhale of every parent who feels the weight of creating a society that puts inclusion and radical love first, and it still takes my breath away. As a mom practicing Social Justice Parenting, I try to be mindful of all of the experiences that I expose my children to, not always successfully. Still, I allow myself to sit in forgiveness, in the place of learning and growing. Parents who live in a place of radical love do not pretend to know all of their children's questions or experiences. Instead, they rejoice in the discovery and the journey together with their child through critical conversation and a strong commitment to reflection. Parenting, whether it's through a lens of social justice or not, is always about making the best decision with the knowledge you have, making mistakes, adjusting, and then readjusting. Remember to give yourself and your children grace and compassion as you do this work together. It does make a difference, I promise you.

There are so many ways to be an advocate and an activist in this world, but I believe Social Justice Parenting may be the one that will have the largest impact. Each generation improves upon the last, and I do believe, as Barack Obama said, that "the arc of the moral universe is long, but it bends toward justice."* But we have to *make* it bend that way. We have to exert the force of our radical love and do the work of our generation, so that our children's generation can do their own work, and so on. This is the only way we will ever reach true justice and equality, and it requires each of us. We need you. You need us. My kids need you, and your kids need you.

I want Social Justice Parenting to offer you hope and direction when you get stuck or you need support to keep doing the work. Let's commit to remaining open-minded and openhearted, to continue to engage in open dialogue, even when it's hard. Let's use radical love armor for action taking, for living with audacity and boldness, not fear and control. Together, let's take risks to change the world for your children and for my children, because together, we can do hard things. We are stronger together. We can raise anti-racist, compassionate, and justice-minded kids in an unjust world. That's the power of this activism, parenting.

---

* Former president Barack Obama helped popularize this quote, which is often attributed to Martin Luther King Jr., who famously spoke these words in 1965 at the end of his Selma-to-Montgomery march. However, King paraphrased this quote from a sermon originally delivered in 1853 by the abolitionist minister Theodore Parker.

ACKNOWLEDGMENTS

I love my village and am so blessed by each member! Thank you to my agent, Lynn Johnston, and my editor, Julie Will, for your guidance and encouragement. You both believed in this book the moment you heard me talk about it. Your support and attention to detail cannot be measured. I am so grateful to you for your time, dedication, and expertise. A special shout-out and thank-you to Tara Parker Pope; it was my conversation with you and your encouragement (and introduction to Lynn) that got the ball rolling on this project!

Thank you to the entire Harper Wave team—Emma Kupor, Yelena Nesbit, Laura Cole, Karen Rinaldi, and Brian Perrin—who answered questions, walked me through the process, and cheered me to the finish line. Teamwork makes the dream work! I also would like to extend my gratitude to Nikki Van De Car of KN Literary, who dedicated time and energy to support my brainstorming sessions that eventually gave birth to the chapters in this manuscript.

My life partner, Tommy, I am forever grateful to you for buckling your seat belt and going on this ride with me. Thank you for trusting me with our family's story. You have been a sounding board, a steady shoulder, and an unpaid researcher. You were patient while I turned my passion into something more tangible that I could share with the world. I love you.

My five heartbeats, Alexandra, Trace, Tyler, Ryan, and Dylan, my greatest joy and by far what I'm most proud of! I will always safeguard your journey, but not from a place of fear. I will always be here to listen to you, learn from you, and love on you. Everything that I do in this life starts with how I can make the world better for you and how we can make the world better for others. May our family's core values and this book serve as a part of my legacy for you, your children, and generations to follow.

To my mother and my three sisters, who are the ultimate examples of radical love, you've always had my back and believed in me. Social justice parenting is the result of what each of you has poured into me all my life. I am so blessed to call you family.

Every woman needs an extended village of sister-friends to remind her that she is enough and to tell her when she is being too much! My sister-friends provide a safe place for vulnerability, trust, and truth. Special shout-outs to my Ride-or-Die College Crew, my sister soul mate, the Dynamic Duo, the Rangers, my BBD Mom Crew, the Rogue Circle, and my DST Innovators. And to Natalie Eckdahl, my business coach and friend, thank you for cultivating my CEO mindset. You all are a constant reminder of what hope and compassion look like and what it feels like to know you belong.

Finally, to the Social Justice Parenting Village, I am grateful to be a part of your parenting journey as you raise children who see and celebrate diversity and who treat others with respect and dignity. You are raising change makers who will disrupt inequities and injustices. The world needs your children, and your children need you. Parenting is activism. Let's continue the work together. We are stronger together.

ADDITIONAL RESOURCES AND SUPPORT

While I hope this book has offered a useful road map for your Social Justice Parenting journey, remember to lean on your village—both local and global—for support and help along the way. If you're a member of a mom group, or if you simply have a few friends with kids around the same age and you share the same values, consider forming a support system so that you always have someone you can turn to when you're not sure what to do or when you need help brainstorming how to handle a certain situation—or even just someone to pick you up when you're feeling discouraged.

There are also a lot of helpful resources available in books and online. (You should absolutely join me and my Mosaic of Moms @socialjusticeparenting on Instagram. The SJP Village provides a space where you belong and are supported!) But I'm going to put my educator hat on and make sure you and your kids aren't just diving into some internet black hole of misinformation that will actually do more harm than good. It's important that your family has the capacity to be critical consumers of media.

That can be a little harder to achieve than it seems. We grew up learning that literacy is the ability to read, write, and think. While this is still true, there's so much more to it these days. Literacy is not just about being able to understand words on a page and writing complete and grammatical sentences—we also must have the ability to understand the different types of media (children's literature, text messages, social media, movies, memes, and more) that our children are exposed to and be aware of the subconscious messages they are sending on a daily basis.

For example, marketers often create commercials that draw your younger children to the television screen. When a commercial comes on, ask your children questions that will help them better understand the intent behind it. Ask your children questions about what they are seeing. What is the commercial about? What is the commercial trying to tell you to do? How does the commercial make you feel? Discuss why famous people and characters are used to sell things that they like. Talk about the way commercials "sell" to them as consumers. When my children were younger, they would see toys or gadgets on television and ask me to buy them. I would ask if they thought the toy would work the same way when they got it home. We would talk about why the people produced a commercial that made everything look like it was hours of fun.

This is just one of the many ways the media manipulates us, and it's a fairly obvious one—but bringing awareness to it will help you and your kids remember to remain aware of the other, subtler manipulations and help to build critical media literacy—which will help our children better analyze what they read and see, and help them understand themselves and the world around them. Being critical consumers of media can also help us and our children challenge many of the -isms (racism, sexism, colorism, etc.) in our society.

Once your kids reach their tweens, you can go much deeper. When my oldest two were tweens, I allowed them to watch some of the tween television shows on the two big children's networks. After watching with them, we began to engage in our own research study and discussed the pattern that we always saw in all of the shows. The main tween character was sneaking, lying, or hiding something, and the parents were always clueless and ill-informed. We discussed these dynamics and talked about how this could possibly cause issues in real life if my kids took those messages as truth and lost their faith in us as parents—and if we, therefore, lost our faith in them as trustworthy people who showed good judgment. It's also a great opportunity to discuss ethical dilemmas and what they would do if they were in the shoes of the main character. Discuss how their decisions align or contrast with your family's core values.

The decisions that children make in their teenage years, specifically on their phones and with social media, can impact the rest of their lives. Set parameters with your children and have an ongoing dialogue about the difference between social media life and real life. There are so many teenagers who feel pressure to look or behave certain ways because of the filters, camera lighting, and fantasy worlds of social media, and these pressures have been proven to have a direct connection to depression, anxiety, and suicide. The reward center of the brain responds to "likes," which leads to the addictive behavior that children display when on their electronic devices.

Because most of our tweens and teens have cell phones, they are constantly bombarded with information. It's important to support them in discerning the difference between real and fake news. Have them ask themselves critical questions such as *Who made this video? What was the purpose of making it? Who does it include and who does it leave out? What point of view is this, or who are they marketing to and why?*

USING CHILDREN'S LITERATURE

Children's books are a great way to begin the practice of critical literacy, and they can be used to support conversations and interactions with your children, which lead to the practice of your values in the world. Books can be used as mirrors, reflecting the lives of the reader. All children need to see themselves reflected in books. Representation matters! Literature adds to their understanding of how they view themselves and how others view and value them. Your children can see evidence of themselves, their families, and communities mirrored in the books they read. This supports their need to be validated and gives them a sense of belonging.

Books can also serve as windows into the lives of others. Literature expands the way your children experience other people's experiences. This is how you can begin to expose your children to differences in culture, skin color, religion, and lifestyle. Children can develop their sense of compassion and care for others while exploring their curiosities about others through the pages of a book.

Finally, books can be used as doors, allowing children to find ways to step into the world of others. If, by peering in through the window of a book about someone whose life is different from theirs, your child is then inspired to befriend someone who is also different, then that book served as a door. Using books as doors can also be symbolic for teaching your children to stand up for others or inspire them to enter other people's worlds through activism, allyship, or volunteering. Children's literature has the capacity to broaden your family's passions and deepen your knowledge of how to use your resources to step into someone's life and to serve others.

However, as much as I believe in the power of children's literature, all books are not created equal. As a Social Justice Parent, it is important for you to analyze the books your children read and the books that you read to them. Begin analyzing the books that you read with your children early in their lives. This will set the foundation for them to do this independently as they get older. I am not asking you not to read books that are controversial or that have been banned for various reasons—in fact, oftentimes those are the ones you and your kids *should* read, together. And regardless of whether you choose to read them, have a conversation around why those books may be problematic for you or for some groups of people. One of our family's favorite "banned" books is *And Tango Makes Three* by Peter Parnell and Justin Richardson. It's a sweet, true story about a male chinstrap penguin couple in the New York Central Park Zoo who raised a baby penguin as their own. This book was banned from various school districts because it was "unsuitable for young children" and has "homosexual overtones."

I want you to explore the books that can be controversial or hotly discussed, but do your homework first so that you are prepared to unpack them with your children. Don't read a book that may have problematic issues and then not engage in the needed conversations around those issues. The Council on Interracial Books for Children suggests ways to analyze children's books for issues like racism and sexism. Some of their recommendations include: look at the illustrations for stereotypes and tokenism, look at the story line for forms of bias, note who the heroes are and who possess the power in the story, and pay attention to any "loaded words" that are used (lazy, docile, savage, etc.).

To help you get started, or to expand your existing library of literature, I've gathered books to represent four age levels: newborn to preschool; kindergarten to second grade; third to fifth grade; and sixth to eighth grade. It is my hope that these books will facilitate important conversations with your children and will support your efforts in raising children who feel like they belong in the world. The following list is categorized by the key themes of this book (belonging, anti-racism, reflection, open dialogue, compassion, kindness, social justice engagement, and self-advocacy). Within each topic, I've categorized by age/reading level. I encourage you to visit your local library or bookstore and bring home some of these books!

CHILDREN'S BOOKS ON SOCIAL JUSTICE

BELONGING

NEWBORN TO PRESCHOOL (NEWBORN TO AGE 4)

It's Okay to Be Different by Todd Parr

   This book teaches young readers to love who they are and to accept and appreciate the differences in others.

The Belonging Tree by Maryann Cocca-Leffler

   When the blue jays and chipmunks moved into the squirrel family's tree, a lesson in inclusion and kindness is needed.

All Are Welcome by Alexandra Penfold

   Imagine a school where—no matter what—you belong.

KINDERGARTEN TO SECOND GRADE (AGES 5–7)

One Green Apple by Eve Bunting

   A young Muslim immigrant starts school in America and immediately feels that she doesn't fit in. A field trip to an apple orchard helps her see the value in being different.

The Big Umbrella by Amy June Bates and Juniper Bates

   With a theme of inclusion and friendship, this special umbrella likes bringing different people together.

A Kids Book About Belonging by Kevin Carroll

   This book introduces children to the concept of belonging, discussing how it feels to belong to a group as well as how it feels when you don't belong, and what to do.

THIRD TO FIFTH GRADE (AGES 8–10)

The Junkyard Wonders by **Patricia Polacco**

Trisha was always placed in the class that was called "special" and thought this meant she wasn't smart. When her family moved to a new town, her teacher, Mrs. Peterson, showed Trisha and her classmates just how special and talented they really are, and how in fact they are marvelous Wonders.

Amina's Voice by **Hena Khan**

This book tells the story of a Pakistani American girl who is stuck between two worlds. In her journey to balance assimilating in America and remaining true to her Pakistani culture, she finds her voice in a way that brings her community together.

The Arabic Quilt by **Aya Khalil**

Kanzi's family has moved from Egypt to America, and she wants very much to fit in. When her classmates see her mother dressed in her hijab, they begin teasing her about being different. Kanzi's grandmother's quilt, which gives her comfort after school, becomes the very thing that teaches the children about inclusion and kindness.

SIXTH TO EIGHTH GRADE (AGES 11–13)

I Can Make This Promise by **Christine Day**

Edie has always felt that she doesn't belong; her mom was adopted by a white couple and no one ever talked about her Native American heritage. One day she uncovers a box hidden in the attic that holds the answers to so many of her questions.

The Unteachables by **Gordon Korman**

The Unteachables, the group of students that nobody wanted, was given to Mr. Kermit, the teacher that didn't want to teach. When a new teacher shakes things up a bit, Mr. Kermit and the Unteachables discover amazing things about themselves and each other.

Listen, Slowly by **Thanhhà Lai**

For the summer, twelve-year-old Mia, a first-generation Vietnamese American girl, was sent to Vietnam by her parents to accompany her grandmother in search of her grandfather. While the trip was meant for her grandmother to connect to her past, Mia finds herself and learns to appreciate her Vietnamese culture.

ANTI-RACISM
NEWBORN TO PRESCHOOL (NEWBORN TO AGE 4)

Skin Like Mine by **LaTashia M. Perry**

This book celebrates the diversity in skin color among young children.

Antiracist Baby by **Ibram X. Kendi**

Kendi shows us that even the youngest kids can combat racism. It's up to us, as parents, to teach them how.

A Is for Activist by **Innosanto Nagara**

This book exposes children (and their parents) to a rich vocabulary associated with activism. It includes terms such as environmental justice, civil rights, and LGBTQ+ rights.

KINDERGARTEN TO SECOND GRADE (AGES 5–7)

The Skin You Live In by Michael Tyler

This beautiful story teaches children about what skin is and what it is not. Everybody's skin is both different and the same.

Something Happened in Our Town by Marianne Celano

The book follows two families—one white, one Black—as they discuss a police shooting of a Black man in their community. It tackles difficult conversations about racial injustice.

Say Something! by Peter H. Reynolds

This empowering picture book explores the importance of using your voice to make a difference. Each of us, each and every day, has the opportunity to use our words and take actions to make a difference.

THIRD TO FIFTH GRADE (AGES 8–10)

Not My Idea: A Book About Whiteness by Anastasia Higginbotham

In this call to action, a young white child recognizes the power and privilege that come along with being white. The child's parents continue to attempt to protect or deny the systemic racism that is happening all around. After a trip to the library, the child uses what has been learned to communicate feelings of frustration to the parents.

Can I Touch Your Hair?: Poems of Race, Mistakes, and Friendship by Irene Latham and Charles Waters

Two poets, one a white woman and one a Black man, explore race and childhood from their own perspectives and lived experiences.

Momma, Did You Hear the News? **by Sanya Whittaker Gragg**

A Black father sits his sons down to share "The Talk" that his mother had with him as a young boy about safe ways to interact with law enforcement.

SIXTH TO EIGHTH GRADE (AGES 11–13)

Ghost Boys **by Jewell Parker Rhodes**

Jerome Rogers, a Black twelve-year-old, is shot and killed by a white policeman while outside playing with a toy gun. As a ghost, he is able to look down on earth and see the impact his death has had on the community. Ironically, the only person who can still see Jerome is the daughter of the white policeman.

New Kid **by Jerry Craft**

Jordan, the main character of this graphic novel, is an African American seventh-grader whose parents enroll him in a private, predominantly white middle school in another part of town. Jordan struggles to find his place between the two worlds of his neighborhood and his new school.

Stamped: Racism, Antiracism, and You **by Jason Reynolds and Ibram X. Kendi**

This book unpacks the history of racism and can be used as a tool for young adults to begin their antiracist journey.

REFLECTION
NEWBORN TO PRESCHOOL (NEWBORN TO AGE 4)

Skin Again **by bell hooks**

bell hooks invites readers to go beyond the color of people's skin and learn their stories and experiences. That's how you really get to know someone.

Fry Bread: A Native American Family Story by
Kevin Noble Maillard

This book highlights Native American culture and the importance of passing down the traditions of their ancestors.

The Wonderful Things You Will Be by **Emily Winfield Martin**

This book represents all the dreams and unconditional love that parents have for their children.

KINDERGARTEN TO SECOND GRADE (AGES 5–7)

The Day You Begin by **Jacqueline Woodson**

This book reminds us that there's power in storytelling. When we have the courage to tell our story, we build the capacity for reflection and belonging.

The Three Questions by **Jon J. Muth**

This is a spiritually-based book that teaches the importance of asking the right questions, living in the present moment, and acting on behalf of others.

Be You by **Peter H. Reynolds**

This book takes the reader through a sweet journey of finding joy in being unique, in being yourself.

THIRD TO FIFTH GRADE (AGES 8–10)

The Memory Coat by **Elvira Woodruff**

This is a story of the journey of a ragged coat and a Jewish family's migration to America. The coat represents the value of keeping family history and memories as part of a collective story passed through generations.

Just Feel: How to Be Stronger, Happier, Healthier,
and More by **Mallika Chopra**

A guide that supports children in identifying, reflecting on, and dealing with various feelings. The reader is given actionable activities that lead to more awareness and mindfulness regarding their emotions.

The Boy Who Harnessed the Wind by **William Kamkwamba**

After being forced to drop out of school because his family could no longer afford the fees, fourteen-year-old Kamkwamba found a way to educate himself and save his village. Through trial and error and persistence, Kamkwamba was able to turn scraps into a working windmill for his village.

SIXTH TO EIGHTH GRADE (AGES 11–13)

Blended by **Sharon M. Draper**

Isabella is biracial girl who is always questioned about her racial identity. In addition, her parents are going through a divorce and she must split her time between their homes. Ultimately, in being forced to reflect on both of her identities, Isabella learns who she really is.

Counting by 7s by **Holly Goldberg Sloan**

Willow Chance is a quiet, eccentric twelve-year-old genius, whose world is turned upside down when she finds out that her parents have died in car crash. In this story we follow her on a journey to find belonging and love with an unconventional family who help her embrace the wonders of being different.

Same Sun Here by **Silas House and Neela Vaswani**

Through letter writing, two tweens with very different circumstances learn about each other's lives. Through their exchange, Meena, an Indian immigrant girl living in New York City, and River, the son of a Kentucky coal miner, discover much about each other and themselves.

OPEN DIALOGUE
NEWBORN TO PRESCHOOL (NEWBORN TO AGE 4)

C Is for Consent by **Eleanor Morrison**

The book teaches children to be in control of their of bodies by learning to say no and creating boundaries for themselves and for others.

We're Different, We're the Same by **Bobbi Kates**

The Sesame Street friends help teach little ones that we all share common traits and experiences, but it's the differences that we should all celebrate.

Brown Sugar Babe by **Charlotte Watson Sherman**

When a little girl doesn't like her brown skin color, her mother reminds her of all the beauty there is in being brown.

KINDERGARTEN TO SECOND GRADE (AGES 5–7)

The Other Side by **Jacqueline Woodson**

Clover, an African American girl, and Anna, a white girl, live in a segregated town. Clover's mom always reminds her to never climb over the fence that separates their backyards. Clover and Anna find a way to become friends in this segregated town while still following the grown-ups' rules.

Let's Talk About Race by **Julius Lester**

This book explores the concept of race for young readers. We are all individuals and we all have a story. Sometimes stories are true, and sometimes we believe stories about others that are not true. When you peel back the layers of our stories, you will find the truth.

The Color of Us by **Karen Katz**

Seven-year-old Lena is going to paint a picture of herself using her brown paint. But as she takes a walk with her mother in the neighborhood, she realizes that brown comes in many beautiful shades.

THIRD TO FIFTH GRADE (AGES 8–10)

A Shelter in Our Car by **Monica Gunning**

Zettie and her mother come to the United States looking for a better life when Zettie's father dies. They temporarily live in their car while Mama struggles to find a job. The book reminds us to remain hopeful in the midst of hard times.

I Dissent: Ruth Bader Ginsburg Makes Her Mark by **Debbie Levy**

Supreme Court justice Ruth Bader Ginsburg spent a lifetime standing up for and challenging gender norms. This picture book highlights her life's work through the lens of her famous dissents.

The Proudest Blue: A Story of Hijab and Family by **Ibtihaj Muhammad**

Faizah recalls the day at school when her older sister, Asiya, wore her hijab for the first time. What started out as a day of joy, pride, and celebration ended in a day of hurt and sadness. This story highlights the importance of family and culture.

SIXTH TO EIGHTH GRADE (AGES 11–13)

Amal Unbound by **Aisha Saeed**

After her mother suffers from postpartum depression, Amal must stop going to school to take care of her younger siblings. Through a series of unfortunate events, Amal finds herself working for the Pakistani village's landlord as an indentured servant.

Long Way Down by Jason Reynolds

After Will witnesses his older brother, Shawn, murdered, he wants revenge. He grabs Shawn's gun and hops on the elevator. The elevator stops on each floor on the way down. Each floor reveals layers of Will's life that led to the moment of Shawn's death.

Other Words for Home by Jasmine Warga

Jude is forced to leave her father, older brother, and her country, Syria, behind during civil unrest. She is sent to live with her uncle in Ohio and she quickly realizes what it means to be a "Middle Easterner" in the United States.

COMPASSION
NEWBORN TO PRESCHOOL (NEWBORN TO AGE 4)

The Rabbit Listened by Cori Doerrfeld

When Taylor's block tower is knocked down, Rabbit is just what Taylor needs. Taylor is able to process the array of feelings inside because Rabbit was willing to listen.

It's Okay to Make Mistakes by Todd Parr

Making mistakes can lead to learning about ourselves. This book teaches children to make lemonade out of lemons and to give themselves a little grace along the way.

The World Needs More Purple People by Kristen Bell and Benjamin Hart

Purple people are people who help others and love who they are. This book teaches children to stand up for what is fair.

KINDERGARTEN TO SECOND GRADE (AGES 5–7)

Listening with My Heart by Gabi Garcia

Esperanza's heart-shaped rock reminds her to show compassion to others. She learns that sometimes she has to use her special rock to practice self-compassion.

I Am Human by Susan Verde

This book affirms the power of giving and receiving empathy and compassion.

Compassionate Ninja by Mary Nhin

Compassionate Ninja teaches young readers the importance of self-compassion and positive self-talk.

THIRD TO FIFTH GRADE (AGES 8–10)

The Lemonade Club by Patricia Polacco

When Marilyn, Traci's best friend, is diagnosed with leukemia in Miss Wichelman's fifth-grade class, they count Miss Wichelman's famous saying "making lemonade out of life's sour lemons" to help them get through it. When Marilyn returns to school after going through chemotherapy, the entire class shows their compassion for their classmate with a sweet surprise.

Fly Away Home by Eve Bunting

The preschool-aged narrator and his father live in the airport while the father looks for more work and an apartment for them to live in. He relies on another homeless family to take care of his son while he is working. This book is an excellent story to support your conversation about homelessness with young children.

Finding Perfect by Elly Swartz

This book is about a twelve-year-old girl, Molly, who has OCD. The coping skills and strategies that were effective in the past are no longer working as her life and the people in it become harder to control. Throughout the story, with the help and compassion from those around her, Molly slowly understands that perfection is not attainable for anyone.

SIXTH TO EIGHTH GRADE (AGES 11–13)

Wonder by R. J. Palacio

Auggie, a ten-year-old who was born with facial defects, is leaving the safety of homeschooling and is going to public school for the first time. This heartwarming story teaches values of compassion, friendship, and standing up for others.

Rules by Cynthia Lord

Twelve-year-old Catherine just wants to be a normal girl and have a normal family. Catherine's brother has autism, and she is often embarrassed by his behavior. This is a helpful book for families with neurodiverse siblings.

Out of My Mind by Sharon M. Draper

Eleven-year-old Melody has cerebral palsy. Everyone sees her broken body but no one knows that she also has a photographic memory. How does she get her her teachers, doctors, and classmates to see her for what she really is? This story teaches children not to judge a person by physical appearance or able-bodiedness.

KINDNESS
NEWBORN TO PRESCHOOL (NEWBORN TO AGE 4)

The Kindness Book by Todd Parr

Being kind is a choice! Parents can use this book to emphasize the importance of choosing to be kind to everyone.

Kindness Makes Us Strong by Sophie Beer

Kindesss can come in so many forms. Read this book with little ones to explore different ways to show kindness.

Kindness Counts 123 by R. A. Strong

This is a simple yet thoughtful book that shares ways to engage in random acts of kindness and to build habits of kindness with your family.

KINDERGARTEN TO SECOND GRADE (AGES 5–7)

Maddi's Fridge by Lois Brandt

Sofia learns that her best friend, Maddi, and her family don't have enough money for food. Sofia is torn between keeping her best friend's secret and confiding in her mother so that they can find a way to help Sofia's family.

Enemy Pie by Derek Munson

Jeremy Ross moved into the neighborhood and he's not nice. At least that's what the narrator thinks. When the narrator's dad agrees to bake enemy pie for Jeremy, the boy invites Jeremy over for the day to feed him a slice of that special pie.

Chocolate Milk, Por Favor: Celebrating Diversity with Empathy by **Maria Dismondy**

It's Gabe's first day of school in America, and he doesn't speak English. Johnny doesn't like the way Gabe talks and decided he doesn't want to be friends with him! This book teaches kids about the values of empathy and compassion.

THIRD TO FIFTH GRADE (AGES 8–10)

Last Stop on Market Street by **Matt de la Peña**

CJ and his grandmother take a bus ride across town on Sundays. CJ sees all the things that are wrong or negative in his community and his grandmother's kind spirit helps CJ see all the beauty in what's around him and to be grateful for what he has.

I Walk with Vanessa by **Kerascoët**

This powerful picture book tells the story of one girl who decided to be an upstander when a classmate was being bullied. This one act of kindness sparks an entire community to do the same.

The Invisible Boy by **Trudy Ludwig**

No one in the class notices Brian and his creative talents until he uses that talent to make the new student feel like he belongs. This act of kindness changes the way his classmates see Brian.

SIXTH TO EIGHTH GRADE (AGES 11–13)

Freak the Mighty by **Rodman Philbrick**

Max and Kevin were always outcasts but found belonging with each other. Their differences create an unbreakable bond as they navigate through life-changing situations.

The Science of Breakable Things **by Tae Keller**

Natalie's mom is suffering with depression and Natalie is desperate to help her. Her last chance is to win the prize money from the science project at school to take her mom to see the cobalt-blue orchids that her mom loves. This is a powerful book to facilitate discussions about mental health.

Pay It Forward **by Catherine Ryan Hyde**

Trevor McKinney's middle school social studies teacher challenged the class to come up with an idea that could change the world. Trevor comes up with a simple plan that transforms his entire community.

SOCIAL JUSTICE ENGAGEMENT
NEWBORN TO PRESCHOOL (NEWBORN TO AGE 4)

Get Up, Stand Up **by Bob Marley and Cedella Marley**

This is a wonderful primer to teach your children to stand up for themselves and for others.

No!: My First Book of Protest **by Julie Merberg**

A toddler using the word "no" can sometimes feel overwhelming for parents. This book introduces little ones to historical activists who used the word "no" to make social changes.

Woke Baby **by Mahogany L. Browne**

This book is a beautiful celebration of toddlerhood and the potential of raising a child who is capable of making changes in the world.

KINDERGARTEN TO SECOND GRADE (AGES 5–7)

Giant Steps to Change the World by
Spike Lee and Tonya Lewis Lee

Children can begin engaging in activism even in the earliest years. Using examples of historical activists, this story presents icons as regular people who stood up for what they believed in and helped change the world, one step at a time.

*The Youngest Marcher: The Story of Audrey Faye Hendricks,
a Young Civil Rights Activist* by **Cynthia Levinson**

Learn about Audrey Faye Hendricks, the youngest activist at a civil rights protest in Birmingham, Alabama.

If You're Going to a March by **Martha Freeman**

This story helps young activists prepare and participate in peaceful protests.

THIRD TO FIFTH GRADE (AGES 8–10)

*Sit-In: How Four Friends Stood Up by Sitting
Down* by **Andrea Davis Pinkney**

This book tells the story of how four Black male college students decided to take a stand by sitting down.

Voice of Freedom: Fannie Lou Hamer
by **Carole Boston Weatherford**

This is an account of Fannie Lou Hamer's life, from her childhood as a daughter of sharecroppers to the last years of her life fighting for civil rights and equity.

IntersectionAllies: We Make Room for All by **Chelsea Johnson, LaToya Council, and Carolyn Choi**

The intersectionality of the nine characters in this story is highlighted and celebrated. This book is a fantastic example of how we can use our privileged identities to support others.

SIXTH TO EIGHTH GRADE (AGES 11–13)

A Good Kind of Trouble by **Lisa Moore Ramée**

Shayla is a rule follower. She feels comfortable with boundaries. But when her sister, Hana, is active in the Black Lives Matter protests, Shayla realizes that sometimes it's important to break the rules.

One Crazy Summer by **Rita Williams-Garcia**

Eleven-year-old Delphine and her two younger sisters find themselves spending the summer in California with a mother that chose a life with the Black Panthers instead of being a mother to the girls in Brooklyn. What will they learn about the mother that abandoned them for the last seven years?

Count Me In by **Barsha Bajaj**

Neighbors Karina and Chris, along with Karina's grandfather, were attacked in a race-based hate crime. Karina and her grandfather, an Indian American, were called Muslim terrorists during the attack. Karina decides to take action in her community.

SELF-ADVOCACY
NEWBORN TO PRESCHOOL (NEWBORN TO AGE 4)

Hair Love by **Matthew A. Cherry**

A Black daddy learns to style his Black daughter's gorgeous curly hair, teaching self-confidence and self-love.

Be Who You Are by Todd Parr

This book shows young children that it's awesome to be the person you were meant to be.

Ella Sarah Gets Dressed by Margaret Chodos-Irvine

Ella loves to express herself by wearing bright colors and patterns and fancy style. Before she leaves the house, all her family members comment on Ella's outfit. Will she listen to them and change her clothes?

KINDERGARTEN TO SECOND GRADE (AGES 5–7)

I Am Enough by Grace Byers

We all want to raise children who are self-confident and who know that they are worthy. This is a great book to begin the journey of self-acceptance and self-love.

Red by Michael Hall

This book teaches kids not to be afraid to be themselves, even when others want them to change.

Amazing Grace by Mary Hoffman

Grace's family tells her she can be anything. So, when a boy at school tells her she can't be Peter Pan because she's Black, Grace's grandmother has something to say about that.

THIRD TO FIFTH GRADE (AGES 8–10)

What Should Danny Do? by Adir Levy

Every choice that you make has consequences. This book allows the reader to help Danny make choices during his day.

Weird!: A Story About Dealing with Bullying
in Schools by Erin Frankel

In this book, young Luisa is called "weird" by her classmate Sam when she is just being herself. We watch what happens as Luisa is supported by her peers to stand up to Sam.

The Thing Lou Couldn't Do by Ashley Spires

In this story, a young girl named Lou learns to change her mindset, stop procrastinating, and face the things she's afraid of.

SIXTH TO EIGHTH GRADE (AGES 11–13)

Brown Girl Dreaming by Jacqueline Woodson

In powerfully moving autobiographic prose, Woodson describes her childhood and growing up Black in America, offering young readers the opportunity to see what it means to fight for justice and equality.

Trout and Me by Susan Shreve

Ben has ADHD and dyslexia. As much as he tries to focus, he often finds himself getting in trouble. Trout learns how he can help Ben be appreciated for who he is instead of being judged by his behaviors.

Bluefish by Pat Schmatz

Travis, an eighth-grader living with his alcoholic grandfather, finds himself at a new school and befriending Velveeta, a popular girl. They both struggle with the weight of family secrets but find comfort and support in their special friendship.

ABOUT THE AUTHOR

Dr. Traci Baxley is a professor at Florida Atlantic University, consultant, parenting coach, speaker, and mother to five children. She is the creator of Social Justice ParentingTM, a parenting philosophy that moves families from fear-based parenting to parenting from a place of radical love. As a diversity, equity, and inclusion consultant, Dr. Baxley supports organizations and corporations in developing inclusive practices and policies that lead to workplace belonging and high productivity.

Dr. Baxley has been an educator for more than thirty years, with degrees in child development, elementary education, and curriculum and instruction. She specializes in belonging, diversity and inclusion, anti-bias curriculum, and social justice education. Dr. Baxley's work has been published in international and national peer-reviewed journals and book chapters. She is the coauthor of *(In)Visible Presence: Feminist Counter-Narratives of Young Adult Literature Written by Women of Color* and coeditor and author on a university textbook project titled *Equity Pedagogy: Teaching Diverse Student Populations*.

You can follow Traci on Instagram @socialjusticeparenting.